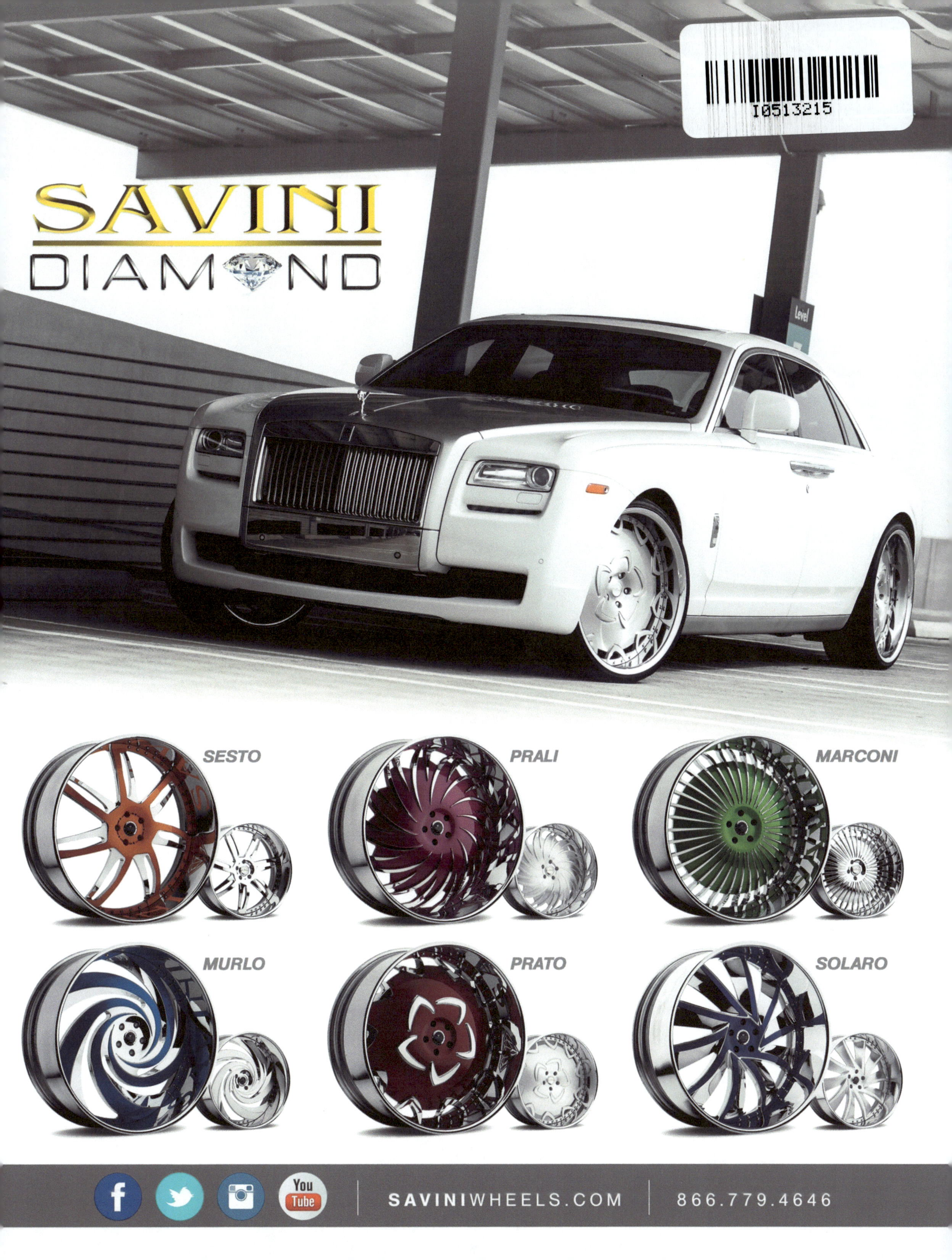

SAVINI DIAMOND

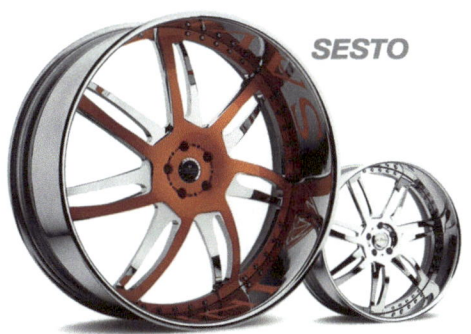
SESTO

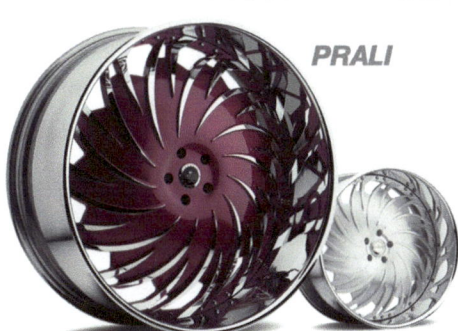
PRALI

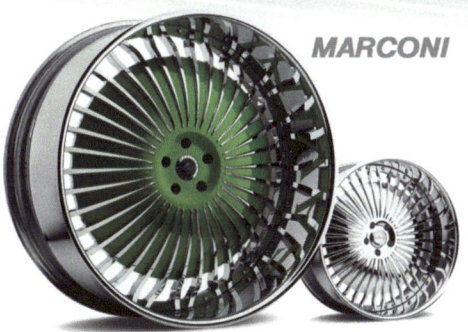
MARCONI

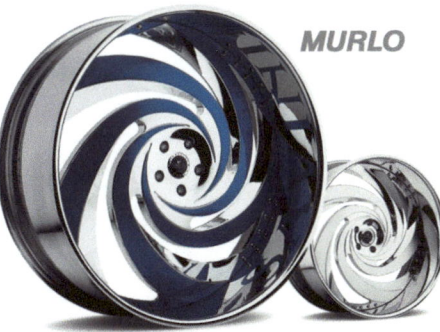
MURLO

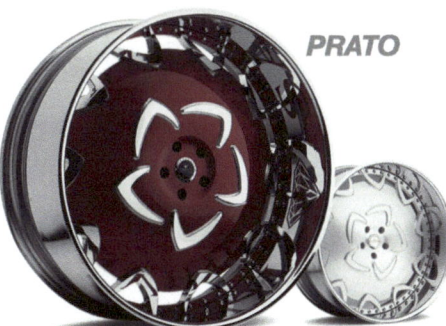
PRATO

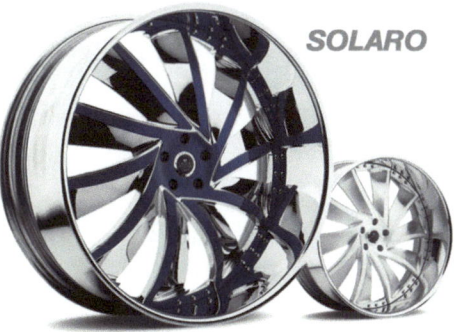
SOLARO

SAVINIWHEELS.COM | 866.779.4646

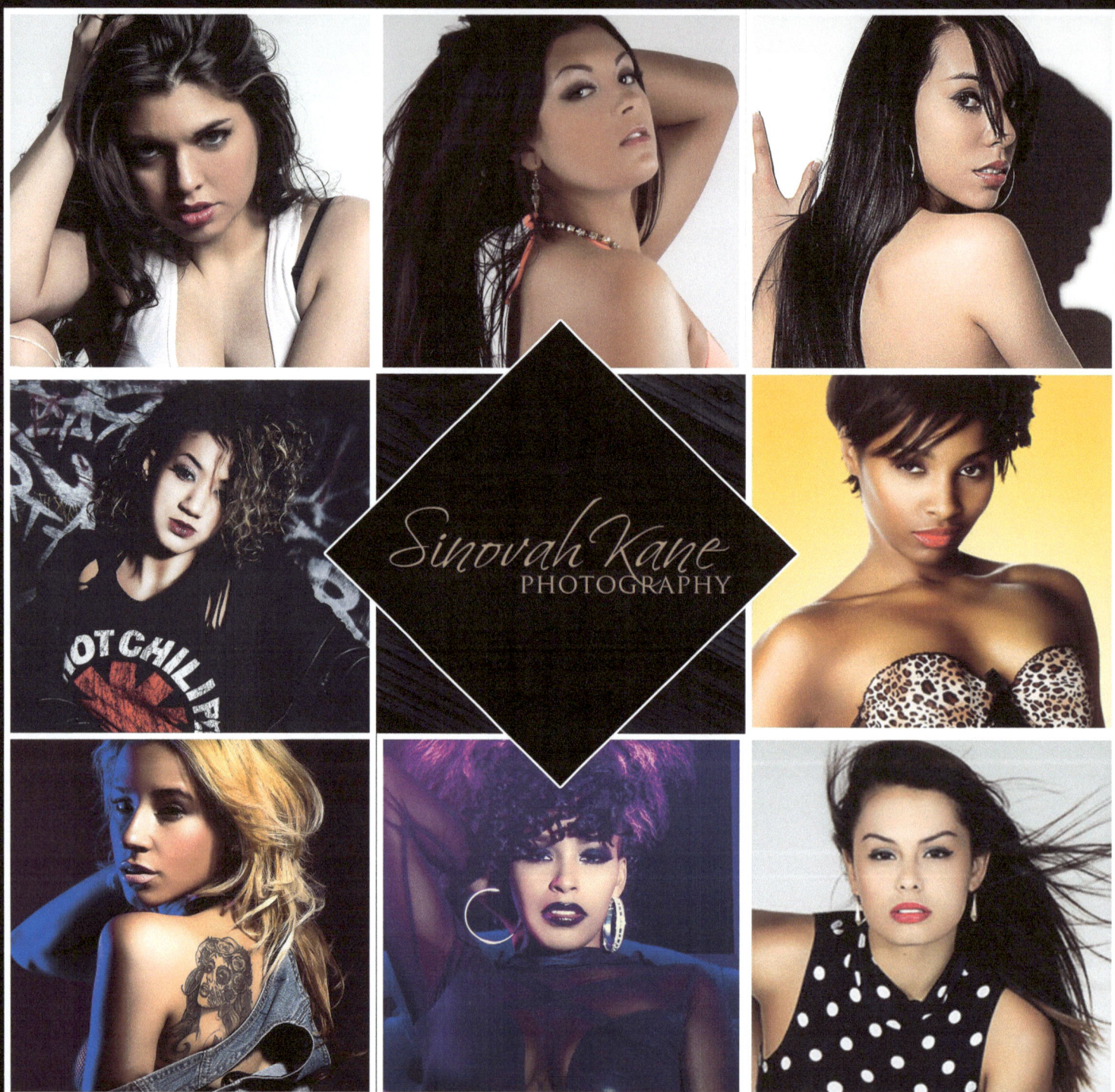

NEFERTITI

pg. 20

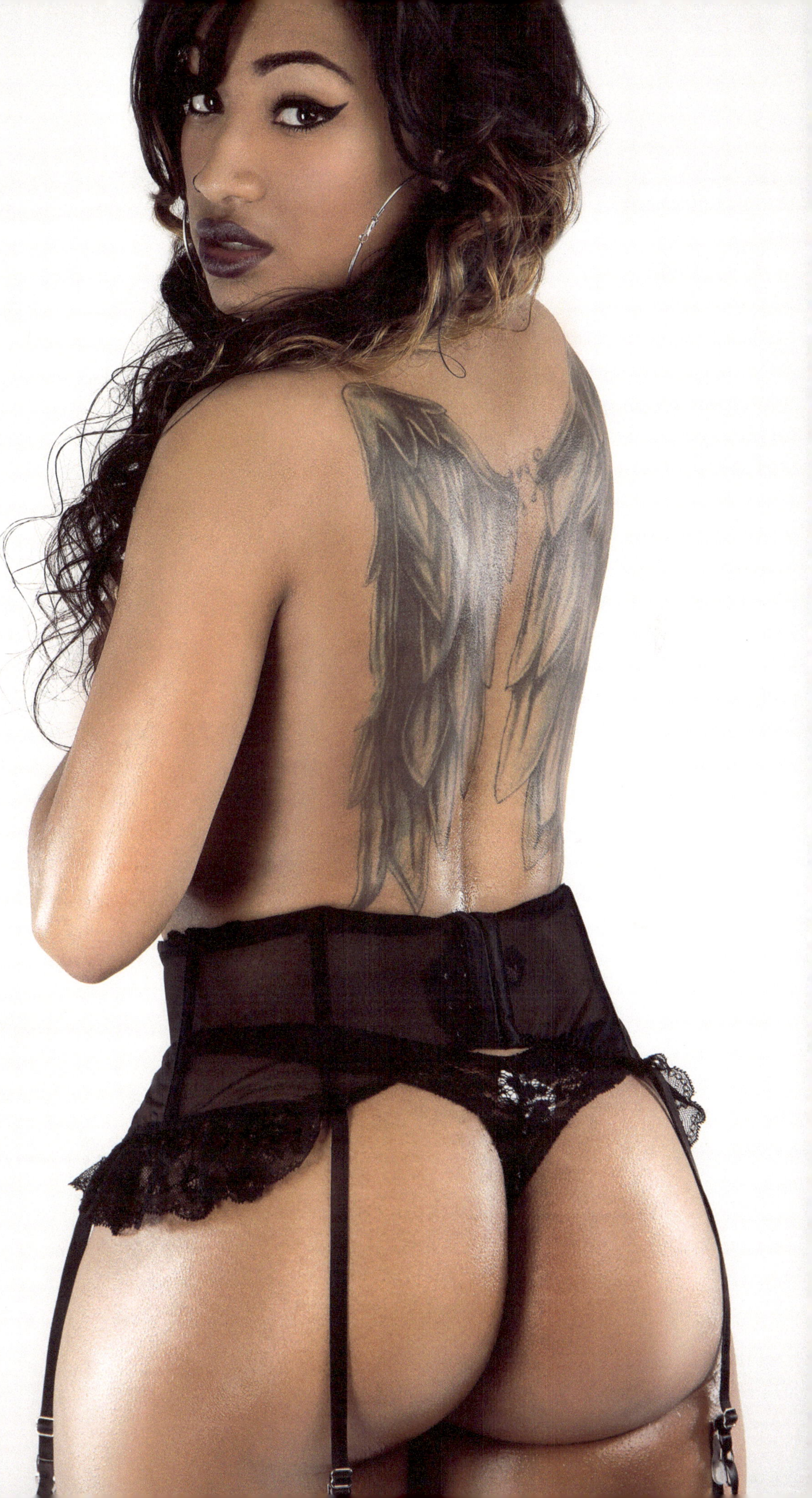

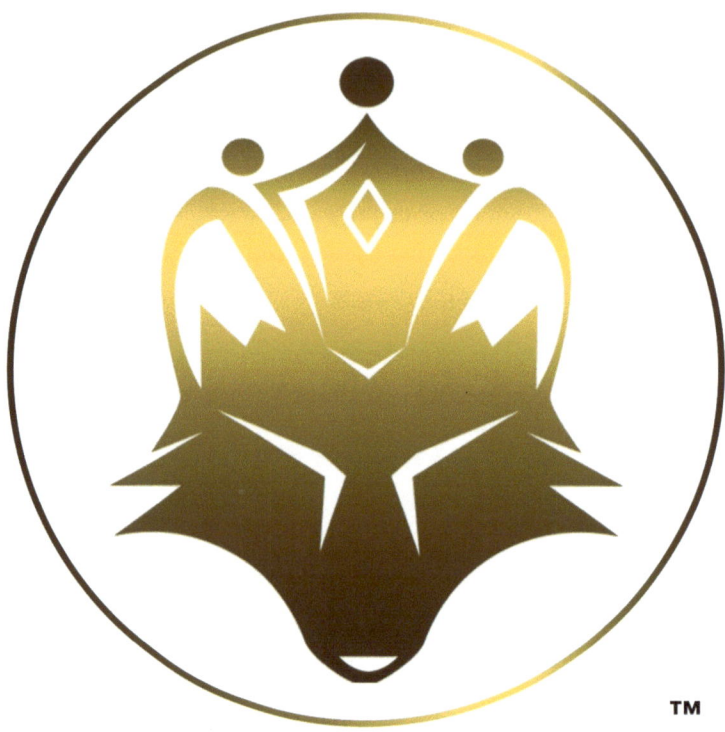

WWW.FOXTAILMAG.COM

FOXTAIL Magazine (ISSN #978-1981-678334), Issue #1 (January 2015), is published bi-monthly by **Foxtail, Inc.**, 945 W. Agatite Ave., Chicago, IL 60640. The subscription rate is $24.95 per year. One-year subscriptions rates: U.S., $24.95; Canada, $54.95; for all other countries, $84.95 in prepaid U.S. funds. Periodicals postage paid at Chicago, IL and additional mailing offices. POSTMASTER: Send address changes to *FOXTAIL Magazine*, 945 W. Agatite Ave., Chicago, IL 60640,. Reproduction or use of any part of Issue #1 (January 2015) of *FOXTAIL Magazine* without the written consent of the publisher is prohibited. Return postage must accompany all manuscripts, drawings or photographs. All manuscripts, drawings or photographs sent to *FOXTAIL Magazine* will be treated as unconditionally assigned for publication and copyright purposes and are subject to the magazine's right to edit and comment editorially. *FOXTAIL Magazine* assumes no responsibility for the advertisements made herein or the quality and availability of the products advertised herein. *FOXTAIL Magazine* assumes no responsibility to determine whether the people whose photographs or statements appear in such advertisements have, in fact, endorsed such products or consented to the use of their names or photographs, or the statements attributed to them. The publisher is exempt from the record-keeping requirements and disclosure statements mandated by 18 U.S. Code, Section 2257 A - C and the pertinent regulations, 28 C.F.R. Ch.1, Part 75, since all of such material falls within the exempted material set forth in Section 75(a) (1-3) of the regulations.

For Advertising Information Contact:
Foxtail Magazine
945 W. Agatite Ave.
Chicago, IL 60640-4044
advertising@foxtailmag.com

FOXTAIL

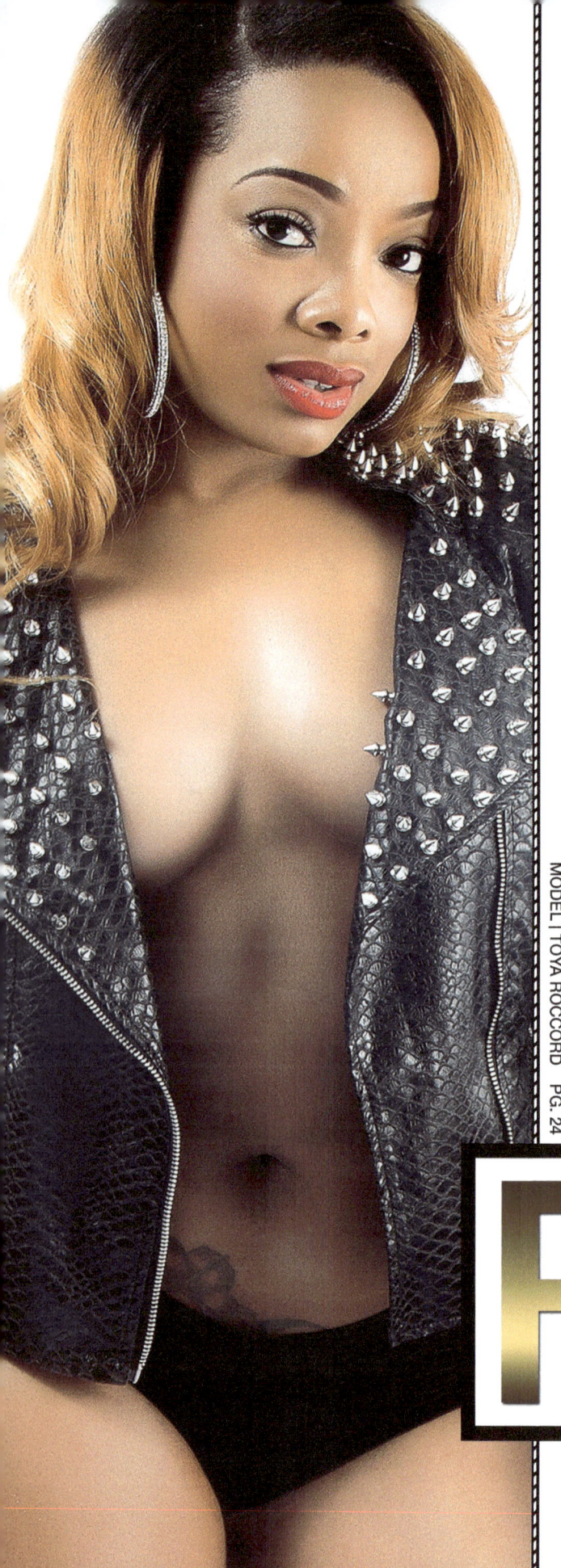

FOXTAIL MAGAZINE
BEAUTY IS LIFE, AND LIFE IS BEAUTIFUL

EDITOR-IN-CHIEF
Charles C. Rigby II
charles.rigby@foxtailmag.com

ASSISTANT EDITOR
Tony Rudd
tony-rudd@foxtailmag.com

SENIOR PHOTOGRAPHY
Sinovah Kane
sinovakane@gmail.com

GRAPHIC DESIGN/PHOTO EDITING
Sinovah Kane Studios
sinovakane@gmail.com

WRITING STAFF
Erika Jackson
Allura Fox
Angie V.

CONTACT
info@foxtailmag.com
modeling@foxtailmag.com
submissions@foxtailmag.com

MODEL | TOYA ROCCORD

FOXTAIL MAGAZINE

WWW.FOXTAILMAG.COM

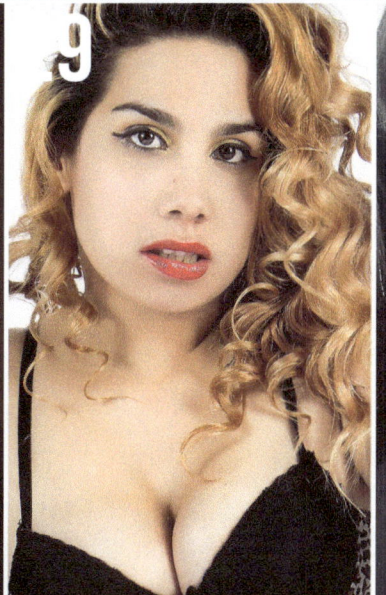
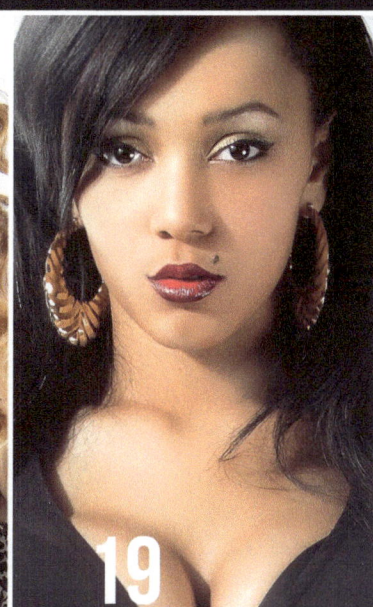
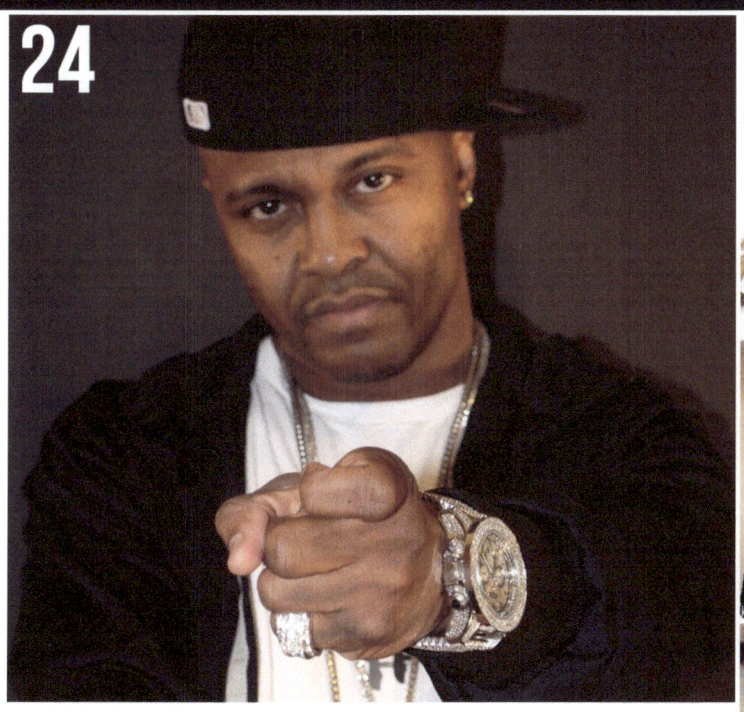
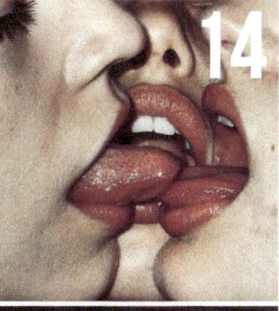
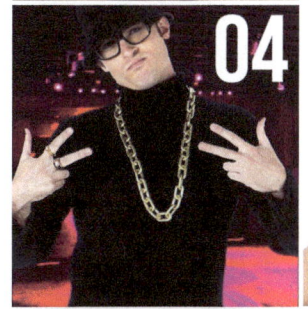
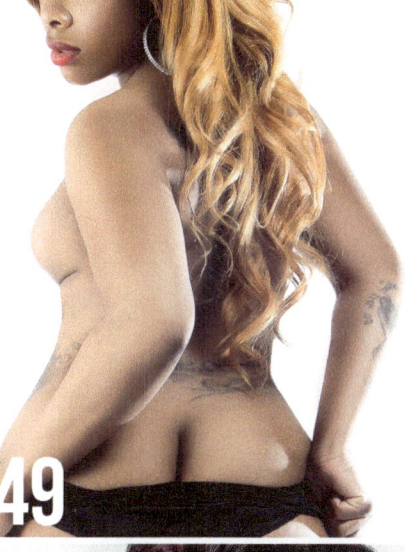
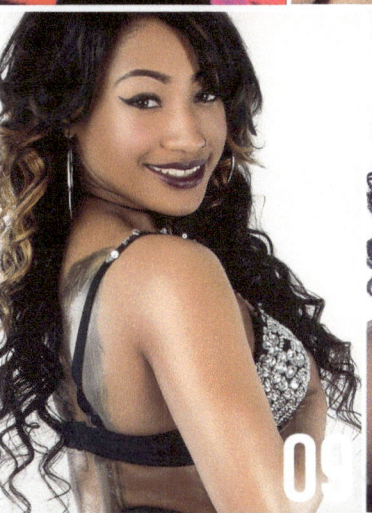
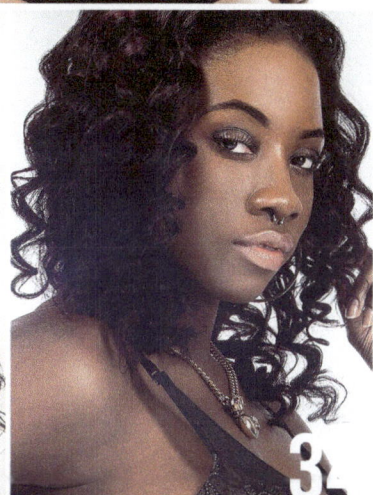

DEPARTMENTS

MAN CAVE	04
THE WHEELS	08
LOOK BOOK	12
SHOE PORN	16
DATING GAME	20
FEED ME THIS	24
REVIEWS	28

FEATURED ARTICLE

ULTIMATE TABOO: HOW TO FIND A SECOND WOMAN FOR YOUR THREESOME FANTASY	39
THE REAL DEAL: BO DEAL	36

FEATURED MODELS

COKANIA	78
ALEIS O'CASIO	24
NEFERTITI	34
THE REAL L.A.X.	24
ASHLEY MARIE	24

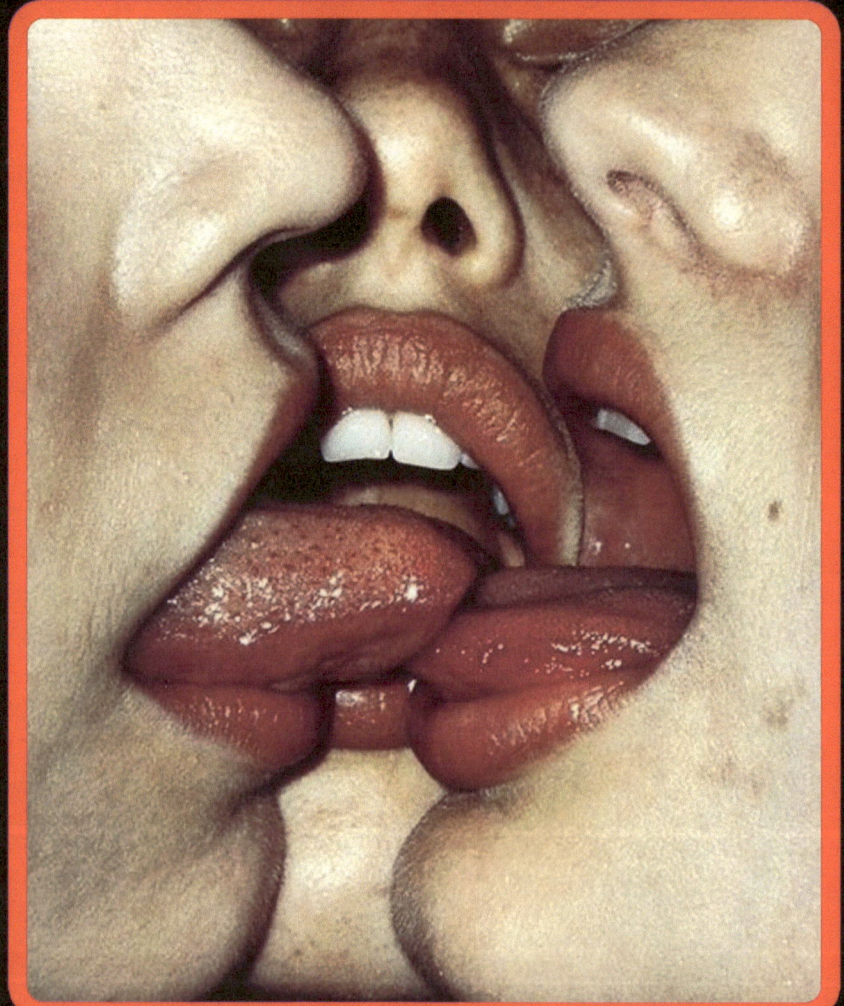

ULTIMATE TABOO

How to Find a Second Woman
to Complete Your Threesome Fantasy

by Allura Fox

ULTIMATE TABOO

So you've always wanted a threesome. Of course you have. You've always wanted to see your woman play with another woman and then share that woman with you. But you've never known how to find a woman to join you and your lady. And such a woman is difficult to find. She's so difficult to find that she's commonly referred to as a unicorn in the swinger and fetish communities. Even though it's difficult to find a unicorn, it's not impossible. I should know, because I was once a unicorn. I'm here to share my experiences and the knowledge I gained therefrom, so that you can use this information to go out and find a unicorn of your very own.

Unicorns Can be Found on Swinger and Fetish Websites

When I decided to become a unicorn, I had no idea what I was doing. I didn't discuss my decision with anyone. There was no way I could tell my judgmental friends I wanted a threesome. I was on my own, guided solely by some sparse information provided by a fellow Reddit user.

As a result of my not knowing any better, I placed an ad on Fetlife.com. Fetlife is heavily populated by people who are into BDSM, which I'm not into, but I decided to give it a try. If I had it to do over, I would have created profiles on swinger sites, such as swinglifestyle.com, lifestylelounge.com, and adultfriendfinder.com. As it would turn out, swingers are more into the type of no-strings-attached sex I wanted and less into the type of kinky, polyamorous relationships Fetlife users prefer.

You should pick a site based upon what type of encounter you want. If you're looking for a girl who's into BDSM or kinky sex, your best bet is Fetlife. Fetlife is full of women wanting to be someone's submissive. Fetlife is also good if you'd like more of a continuous relationship. Fet life users have people with whom they are play partners, polyamorous, protecting, among other various forms of relationship.

Swingers, on the other hand, are monogamous people, who enjoy sex outside the bounds of their marriages. They like to keep things friendly and very casual. Although I've encountered one unicorn who wanted a polyamorous relationship on a swinger site, generally speaking, you're more likely to find a unicorn who doesn't want to be a permanent part of your relationship if you look on swinger sites.

Don't Contact a Unicorn Unless You're Ready to Meet

I thought picking a couple would be easy. I'd be flooded with replies, I'd exchange a few messages with a couple, and arrange to meet them shortly thereafter. Unicorns are so scarce that I thought I wouldn't have to deal with the flakiness that is typically associated with any kind of online dating.

And yet I did. Just as in online dating, there were people who would send me a dozen Fetlife messages, but who would not go as far as to give me their phone number, let alone set a time to actually meet. If I gave someone my number or heaven forbid, asked to meet, all communication would suddenly cease. I soon surmised that those were men whose wives or girlfriends knew nothing about me.

And then there were my texters. Just as in online dating, there were couples who wanted to text me forever without setting a date to meet. I chose a couple early on who turned out to be the type who just wanted to text. Finally, about two weeks after they first began texting me, they finally and very dramatically texted, "we are ready to speak on the phone." They told me when they wanted me to call. And so I called. No one answered. No one called me back. I got an apology text the next day in which they claimed to have fallen asleep at 7:00. I'd heard that same excuse from many of the bad boys I dated off OKCupid. I lost interest after that.

If you want to meet a unicorn, you can't string her along with a dozen messages. Send a few messages, see if you're on the same page, and if you are, ask to meet her, or at the very least Skype with her. The couple I hooked up with didn't string me along with dozens of messages and texts. The female of the couple exchanged a few messages with me on Fetlife, got my number, and asked to meet me. We met, I liked them, and we decided to set a date for sex. Meeting is a step that must be taken if you ever expect to have a threesome.

When You Reach Out to a Unicorn, Show that You're Interested in Her as a Person

The couples with whom I got the closest were those couples who asked me how my search was going or commented about specific aspects of my profile. Since I was new, I received a couple of messages from people who purported to want to help me. They positioned themselves as the people I could go to for advice, which I did. They subsequently transitioned smoothly from giving advice to offering to be the couple I chose. I agreed, because they showed an interest in how I was feeling and made me feel like more than just a sexual object.

After you've shown her that you truly care about her feelings, don't then blow it by going into great detail about how sexually gifted you are. No woman responds to an egotistical guy. The topic of sex can be broached in generic terms which let her know that meeting you and your woman will be worth her while. Instead of bragging, say, "I believe that everyone should have a good time."

Meet During a Time That Could Lead to Sex

When I began my journey, I envisioned one wild night. A night on which we'd meet, and if everything went well, engage in a little play. Sadly, no one else shared my vision. I couldn't convince a couple to meet me on a Saturday night to save my life.

ULTIMATE TABOO

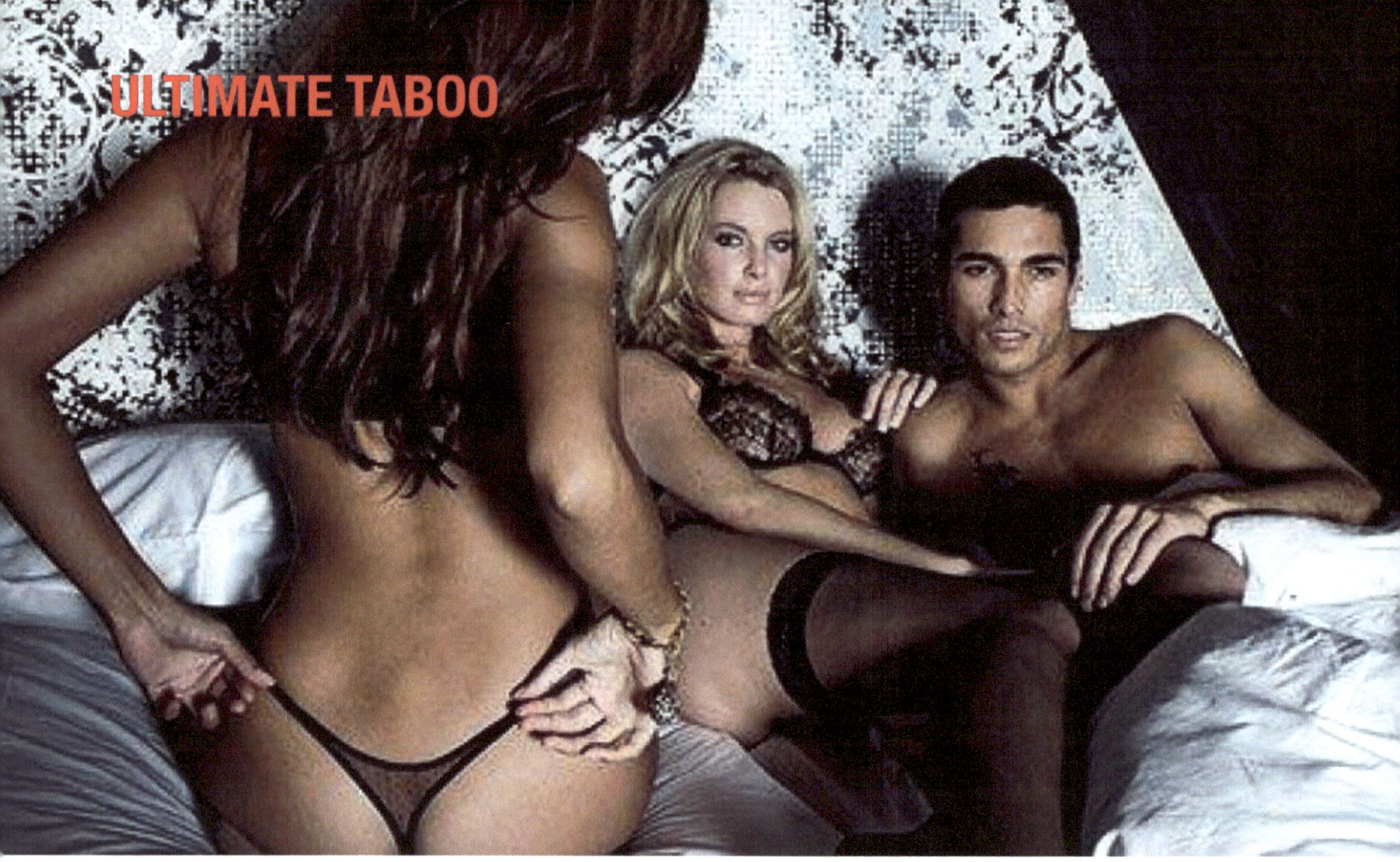

Meet During a Time That Could Lead to Sex

When I began my journey, I envisioned one wild night. A night on which we'd meet, and if everything went well, engage in a little play. Sadly, no one else shared my vision. I couldn't convince a couple to meet me on a Saturday night to save my life. No, they'd want to meet for Sunday brunch or during the hour they had free before they met up with friends. I felt very low on everyone's priority list.

Even though I was hoping for a one night stand, I wasn't opposed to a no pressure meeting first. I just didn't like feeling as if I was being squeezed into a couple's busy schedule. The couple I hooked up with held a meet and greet first, but they reserved an entire night for me. We drank and had a good time getting to know each other, which was much better than when I had to sit with a couple who kept glancing at their watches as they waited for their friends to arrive.

Don't Make Her Feel like She's Auditioning for You

I met one couple I really liked, but ultimately, I couldn't leap over all the hurdles they placed in front of the finish line. First, we had a meeting that lasted a couple of hours at which I "said all the right things." Then, the husband told me I had to start texting his wife, who was completely dismissive when I did text her, and I had to have a date alone with her. I declined, explaining that I didn't feel like I should have to romance his wife. I did go on another day date with them, because I did like them and felt too invested to walk away. It was only after that date that they decided that I was worthy of a threesome with them. Even then, it took them forever to set a date for sex and when they finally did set a date, they subsequently cancelled. I reunited with my boyfriend before they got a chance to reschedule.

Contrast my experience with that couple with the experience I had with the couple I did hook up with. We had one meet and greet before we had sex. I'm not the only unicorn who prefers to have only one meet and greet before hooking up. I spoke to another unicorn who agreed, one meeting is fine, multiple meets is not. No unicorn wants to be strung along for months while you decide if she's worthy enough to be with you.

Leave Her Satisfied and Wanting More

A common complaint among women who have been the third is the mediocre sex. More than one unicorn has complained that she felt like a couple's sex toy. The couple was focused on their own pleasure and used the unicorn to enhance their pleasure, but neglected their unicorn. You have to worry about pleasing both women. You have to make sure neither woman feels neglected. It's not difficult for both women to experience pleasure at the same time. Just use your imagination. If you leave your unicorn satisfied, she might come back for more.

I hope my advice helps you on your journey. I realize that some people might find my advice hard to swallow. A lot of couples believe that a unicorn should jump through whatever hoops they throw in front of her, because she should understand that the couple's relationship comes first. Unicorns should be happy they're being considered for a spot in the couple's bed. This simply isn't reality. I featured excerpts of my article on a swinger forum. I found the division of opinion hilarious. Those who agreed with me were couples who had success finding a unicorn. Those who were angry were couples who had not. So, you can either follow my advice and see your wildest dreams come true or you can keep your fantasy life a fantasy. The choice is yours.

THE REAL DEAL

BO DEAL

BOSS OF CHICAGO

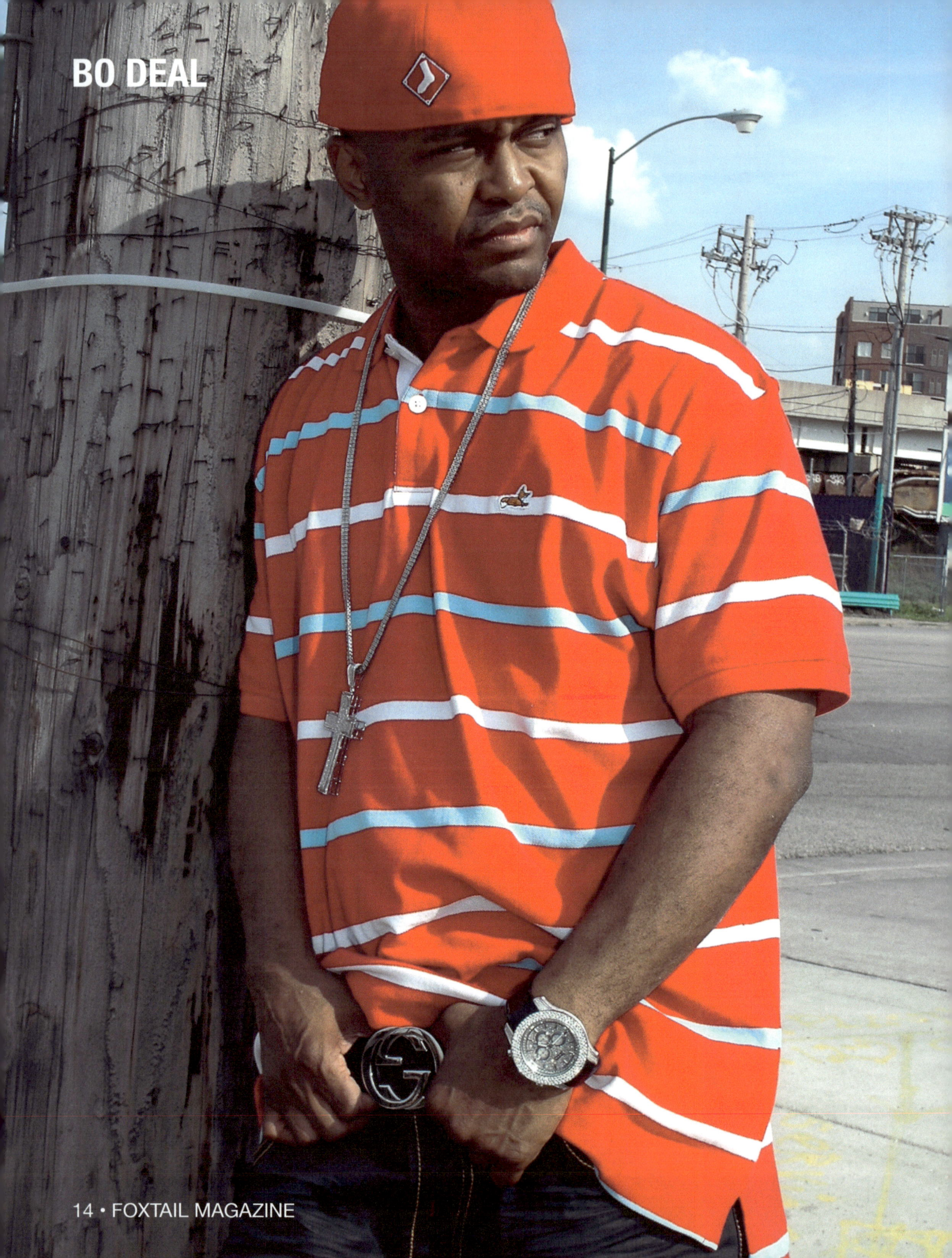

THE REAL DEAL
BO DEAL
BOSS OF CHICAGO

by Tony Rudd

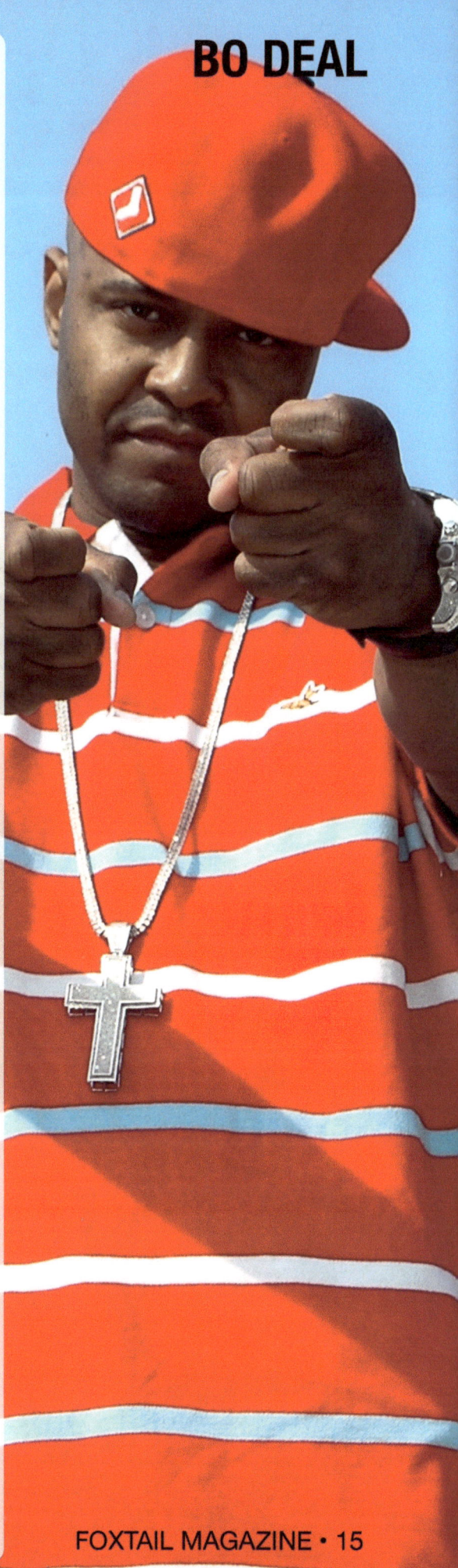

Bo Deal's skills are evident in his work; He prevailed as champion for five weeks on BET's 106 & Park Free Style Friday. His single Murda has 1.5 million views and counting on you tube. Although Bo's style is more hardcore rap, he does cater to his ladies as well. His single Outta Dem Clothes is gaining rapid popularity and is proof of his versatility at attracting a diverse fan base. Bo's current single "Wow" ft Waka Flocka, Twista, French Montana, Trae the Truth and PaperBoy is set to be released on MTV. Bo Deal has several mix tapes that can be downloaded for free from datpiff and livemixtapes websites. He is currently working on Welcome to Klanville mix tape which is set to be released in October 2012.

Bo Deal was born and raised on the West Side of Chicago, where he still resides, in a single family household, with a mother who worked very hard to provide for her children with everything that they wanted and needed, but for Bo that wasn't enough. So came the temptation of the streets and he formed his own clique. The streets of Chicago are intense and riddled with crime, as it is famously called Chi-raq. Bo being the soldier he has equipped himself for whatever the streets could bring his way, this landed him in jail at the tender age of fifteen. Bo had a few run-ins with the law, but the birth of his children was the driving force that nudged him to turn his life around. Bo is very family orientated, he strives to be a better son, father and person every day.

BO DEAL is adorned as Boss of Chicago. He has a style of his own. From the sound of his music, you can tell he was born to do this. Bo appears like the typical rap mogul in his attire, but after a conversation with him, you will find there is more to him than his bad boy persona. Bo is a modest and kind individual; he encourages unity among his fellow artists and Diaspora of people. Bo Deal started having problems with the law in his teenage years because of his prior lifestyle, while incarcerated he started to fuel his energy into more positive things like music. He uses his past experiences to teach young men to make better choices. Bo leads by example, he gives back to his community, helping the less fortunate and always willing to lend a helping hand to someone in need.

Bo Deal hosts an annual Back to School Picnic and Fun day, where he gives out backpacks filled with school supplies to children in his West-Side neighborhood. Bo is also involved with the Alpha House, it's a program that teaches young men to make music, and this curriculum serves as an outlet and an alternative for these young men who have had problems with the law. He also helps to transition family, friends and colleagues who have been incarcerated by assisting in funds to buy clothes and necessities upon their release. Bo acts of kindness are endless, and he rarely speaks of them.

Bo Deal's drive is impetus; he is a perfectionist at whatever he does. There is no doubt that Bo Deal is talented, and he works very hard, he is compelled to let his gift be known. While the music industry can change people for the worst, it's obvious that Bo is very aware of the downfalls of the music business and he is determined to stay grounded. Bo Deal's music is addictive, his beats will have you bobbing your head and his impeccable gift, to play on words will demand your immediate attention. He has a tight grip on this music industry and he is a force to be reckoned with. Bo Deal is already a household name in Chicago and expanding to several cities nationwide.

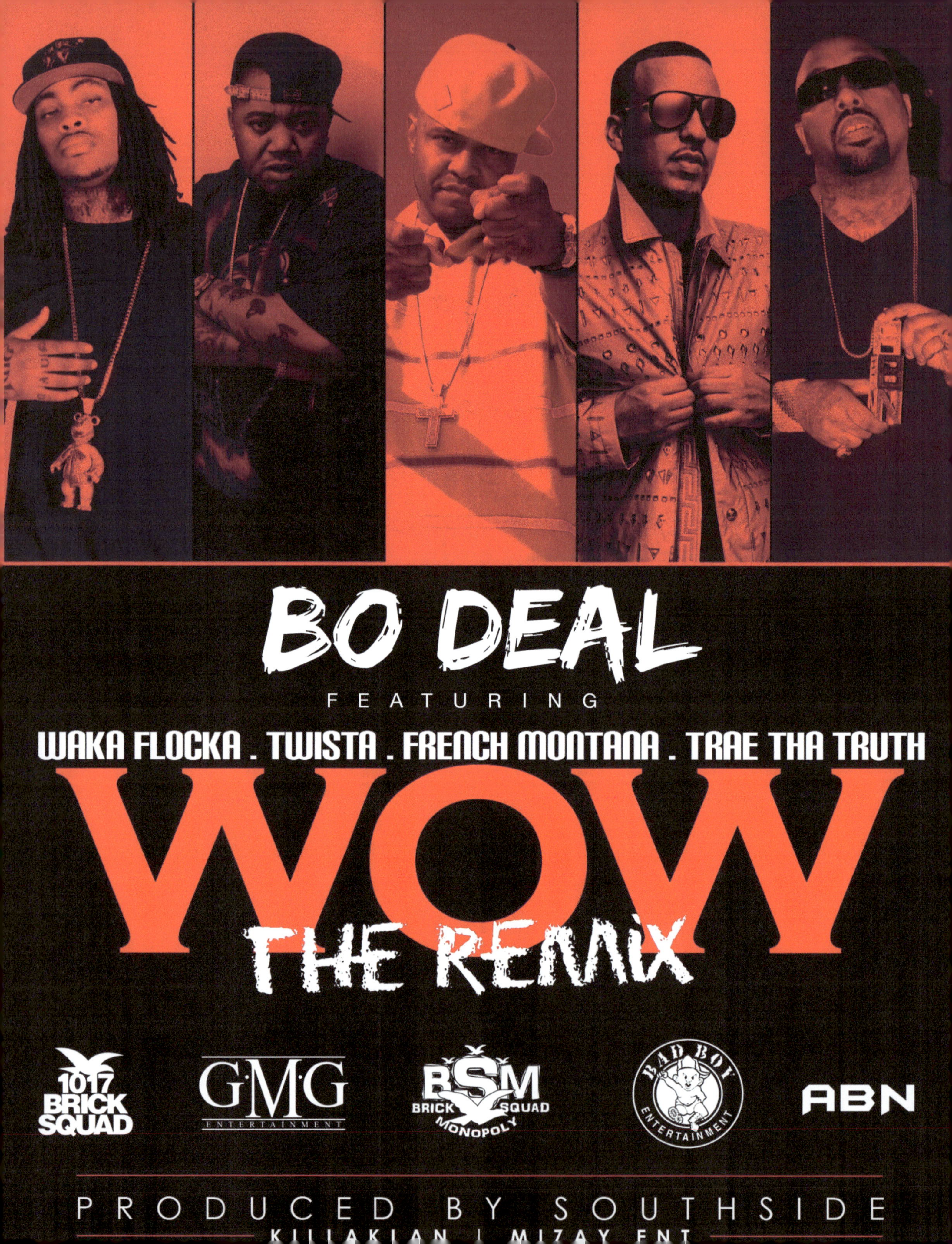

BO DEAL

FEATURING
WAKA FLOCKA . TWISTA . FRENCH MONTANA . TRAE THA TRUTH

WOW
THE REMIX

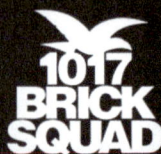 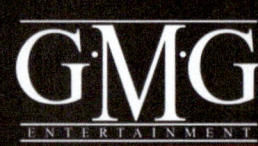 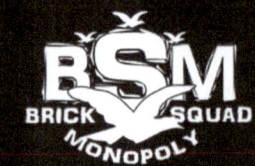 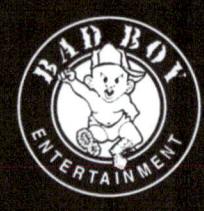 ABN

PRODUCED BY SOUTHSIDE
KILLAKIAN | MIZAY ENT

URBAN MARKETING • MUSIC MANAGEMENT • BOOKING AGNECY

I AM 3230

(708) 557-3230 • WWW.IAM3230.COM

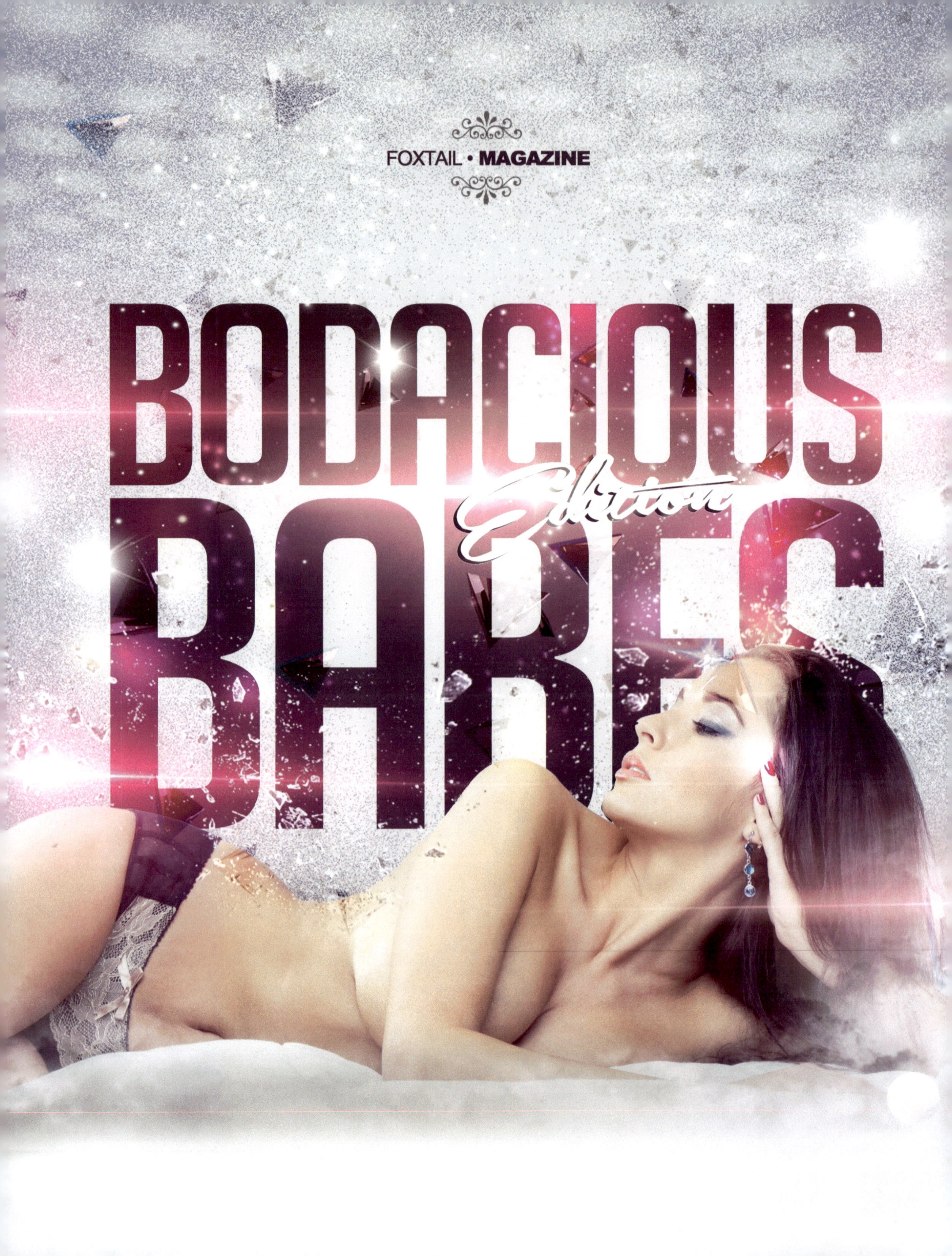

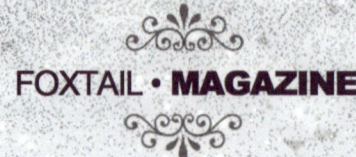

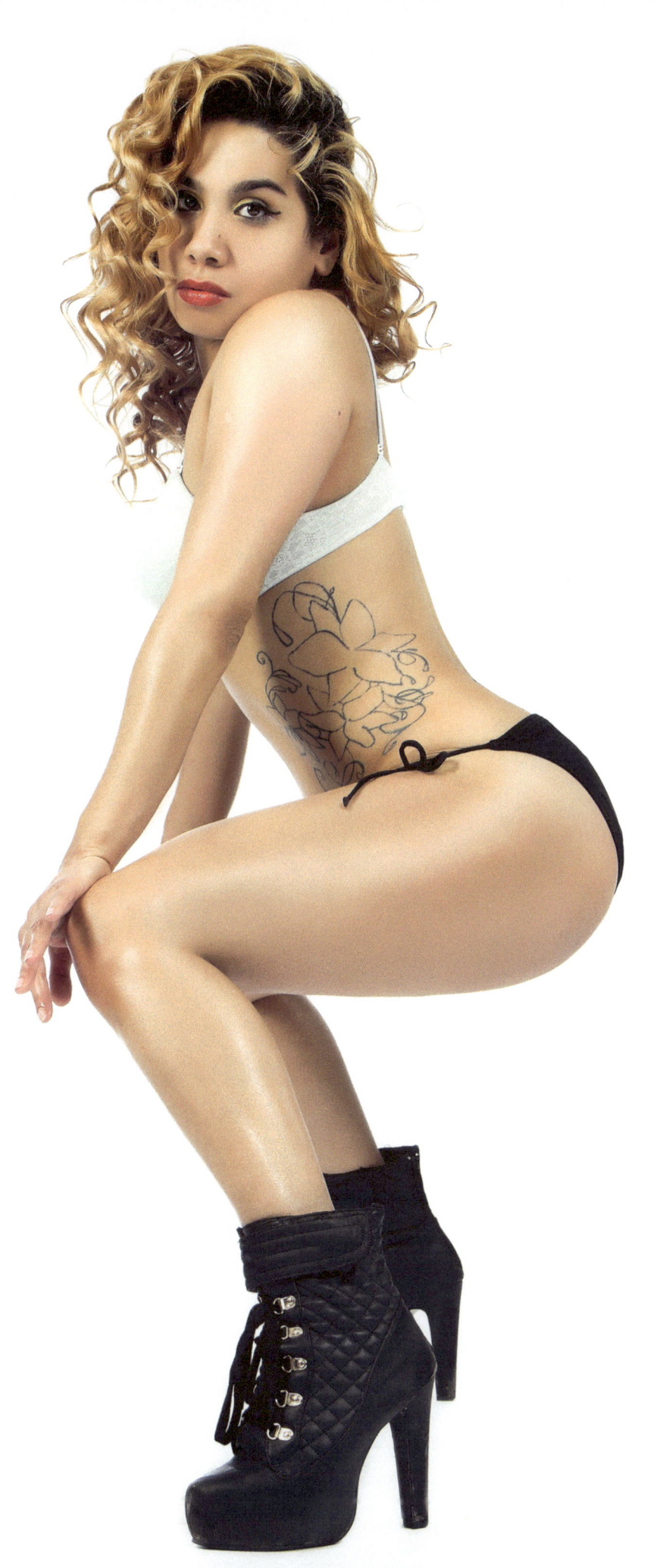

ALEXANDNA OCASIO

PHOTOGRAPHY BY SINOVAH KANE

HEIGHT • 5' 4"
WEGHIT • 128 LBS.
HAIR • BLONDE
EYE COLOR • BROWN
BUST • 38 B
WAIST • 24
HIPS • 36

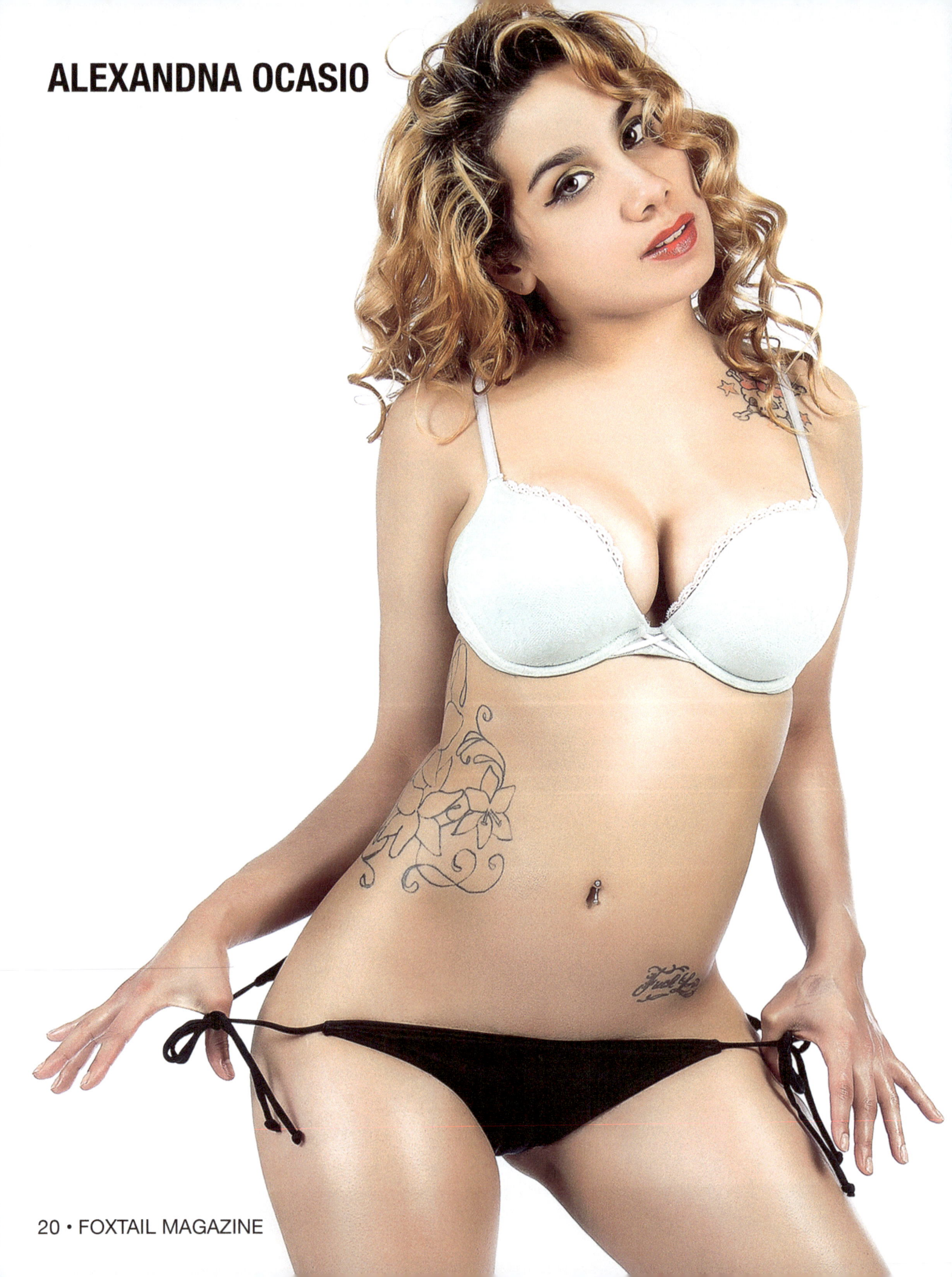

ALEXANDNA OCASIO

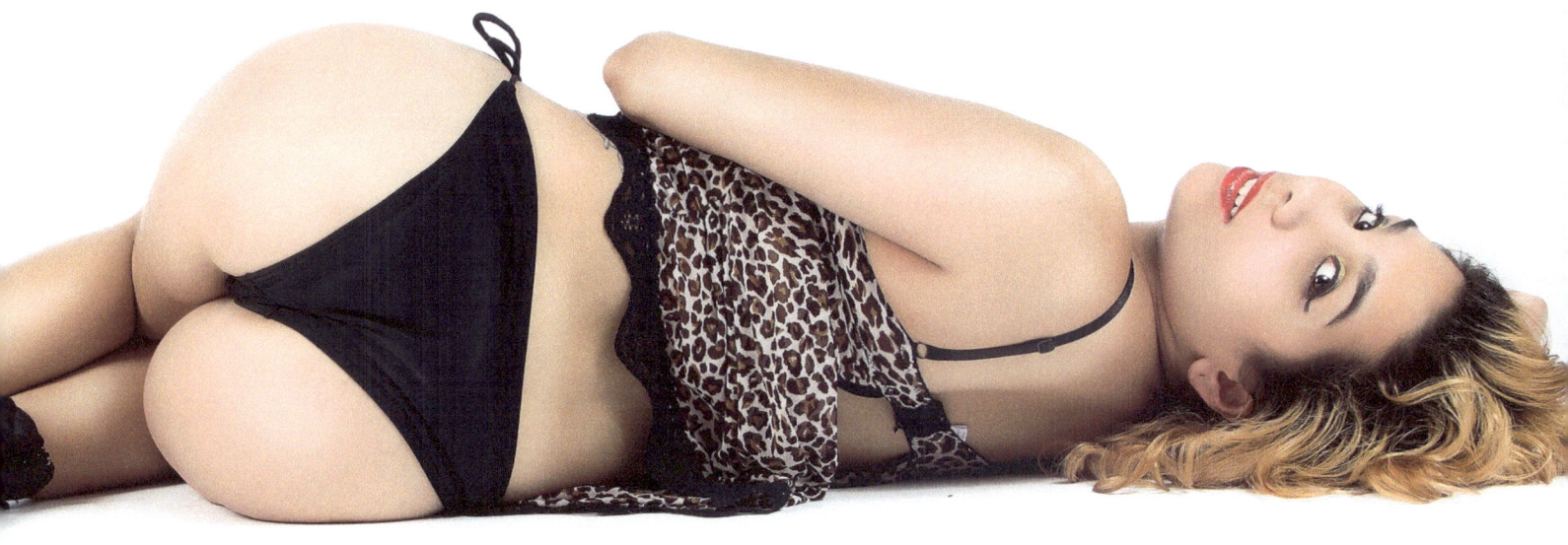

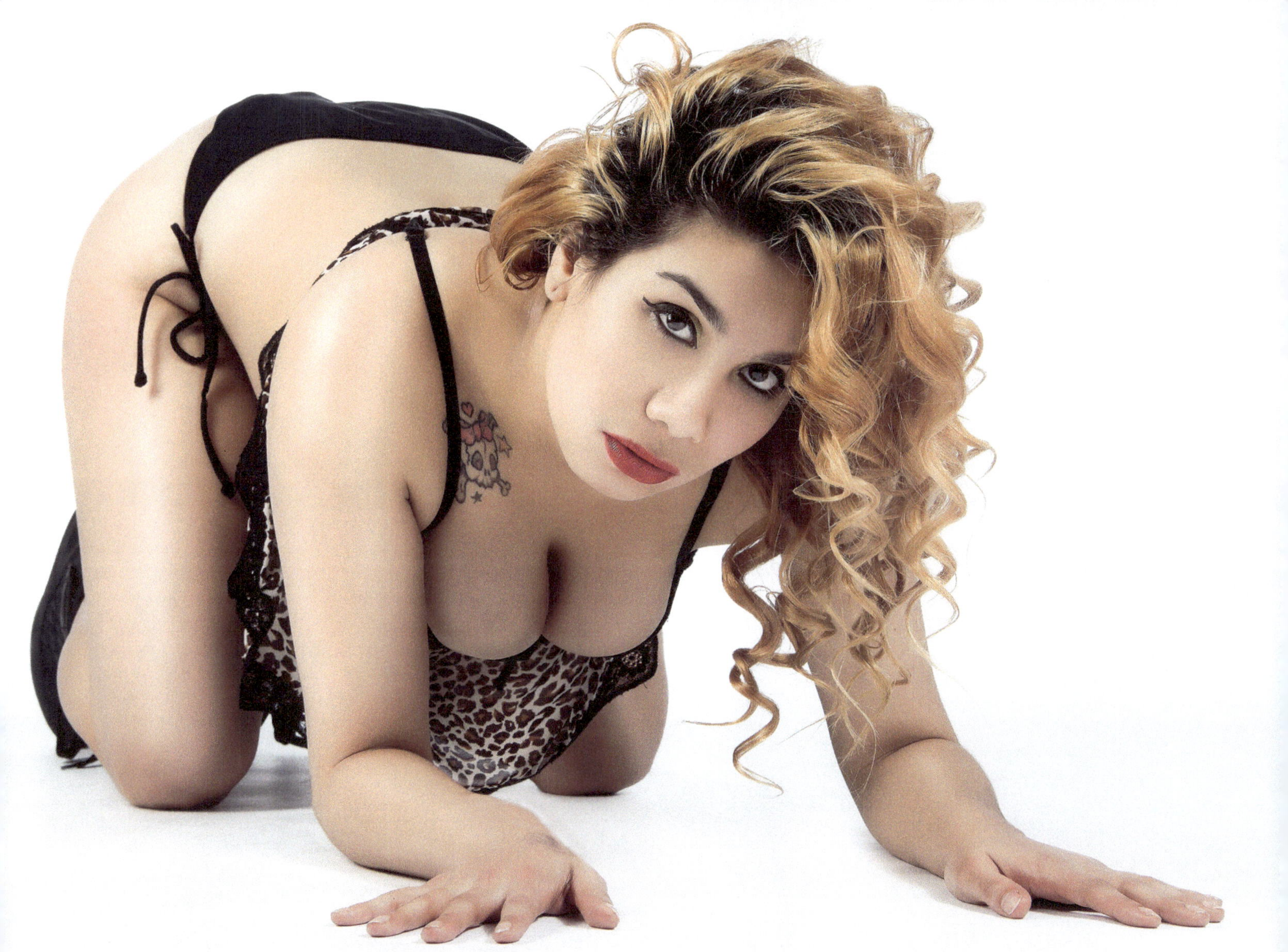

NEFERTITI

PHOTOGRAPHY BY SINOVAH KANE

Age • 21
Nationality • African American
Place of Birth • Kankakee, IL
Where do you rep? • Chi-Town
Height • 5'4"
Weight • 150 lbs.

Instagram • illest_balive
Twitter • _PilotB

Profession • Currently a Student
Relationship Status • Single
Measurements • 34B- 28 - 42

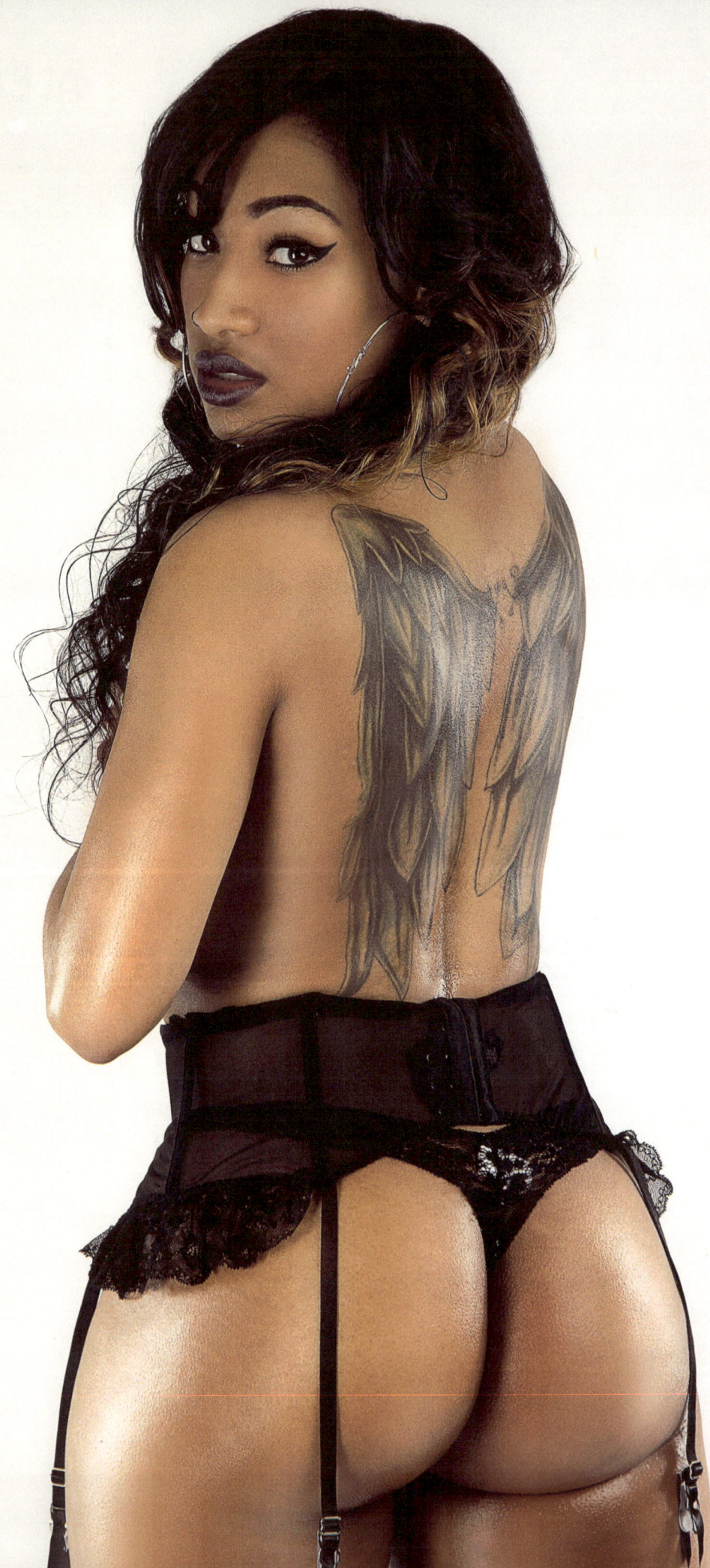

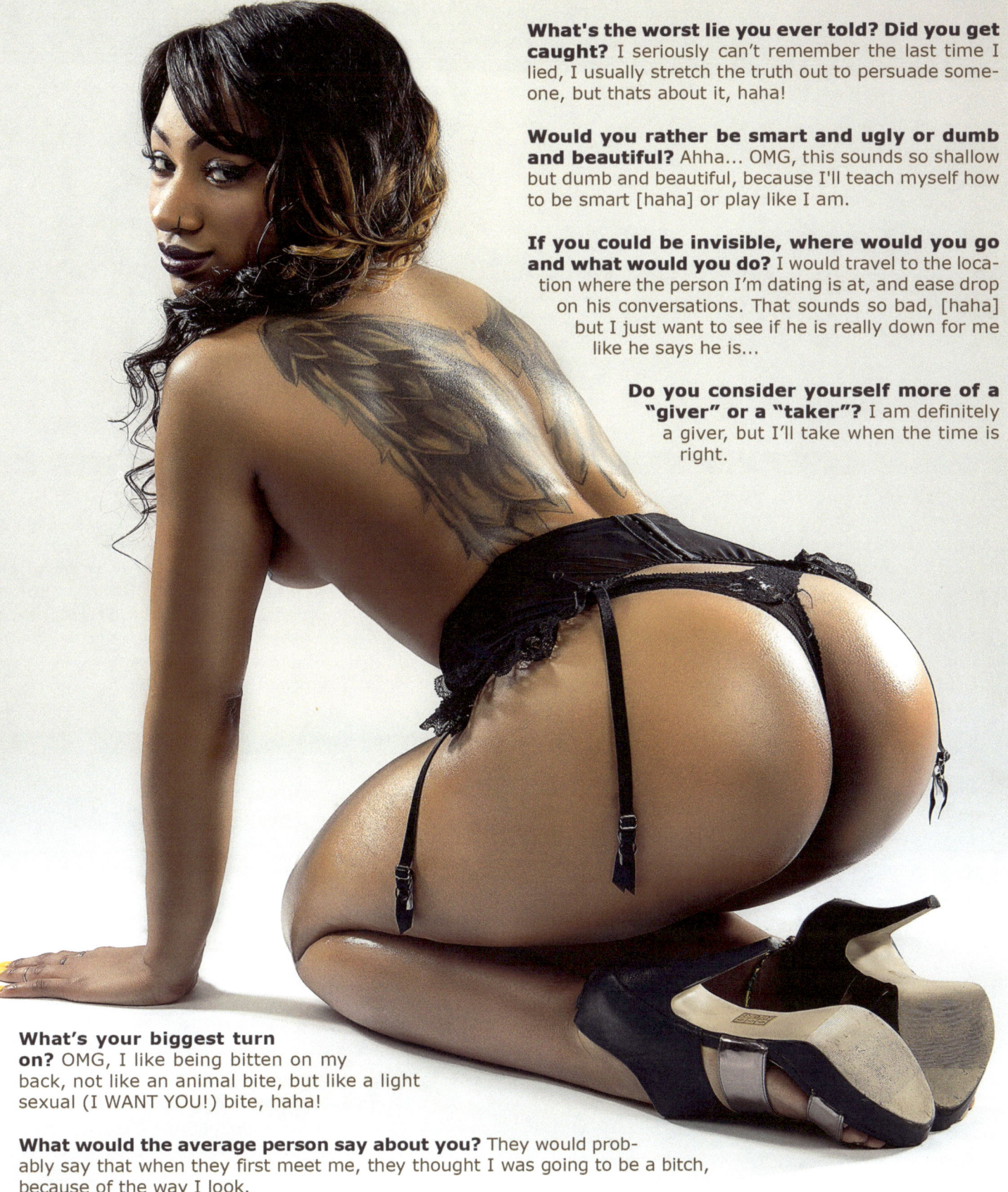

NEFERTITI

What's the worst lie you ever told? Did you get caught? I seriously can't remember the last time I lied, I usually stretch the truth out to persuade someone, but thats about it, haha!

Would you rather be smart and ugly or dumb and beautiful? Ahha... OMG, this sounds so shallow but dumb and beautiful, because I'll teach myself how to be smart [haha] or play like I am.

If you could be invisible, where would you go and what would you do? I would travel to the location where the person I'm dating is at, and ease drop on his conversations. That sounds so bad, [haha] but I just want to see if he is really down for me like he says he is...

Do you consider yourself more of a "giver" or a "taker"? I am definitely a giver, but I'll take when the time is right.

What's your biggest turn on? OMG, I like being bitten on my back, not like an animal bite, but like a light sexual (I WANT YOU!) bite, haha!

What would the average person say about you? They would probably say that when they first meet me, they thought I was going to be a bitch, because of the way I look.

What do guys compliment you most on? My ass, my eyes, and how down I am for them when they are in need.

FOXTAIL MAGAZINE • 23

NEFERTITI

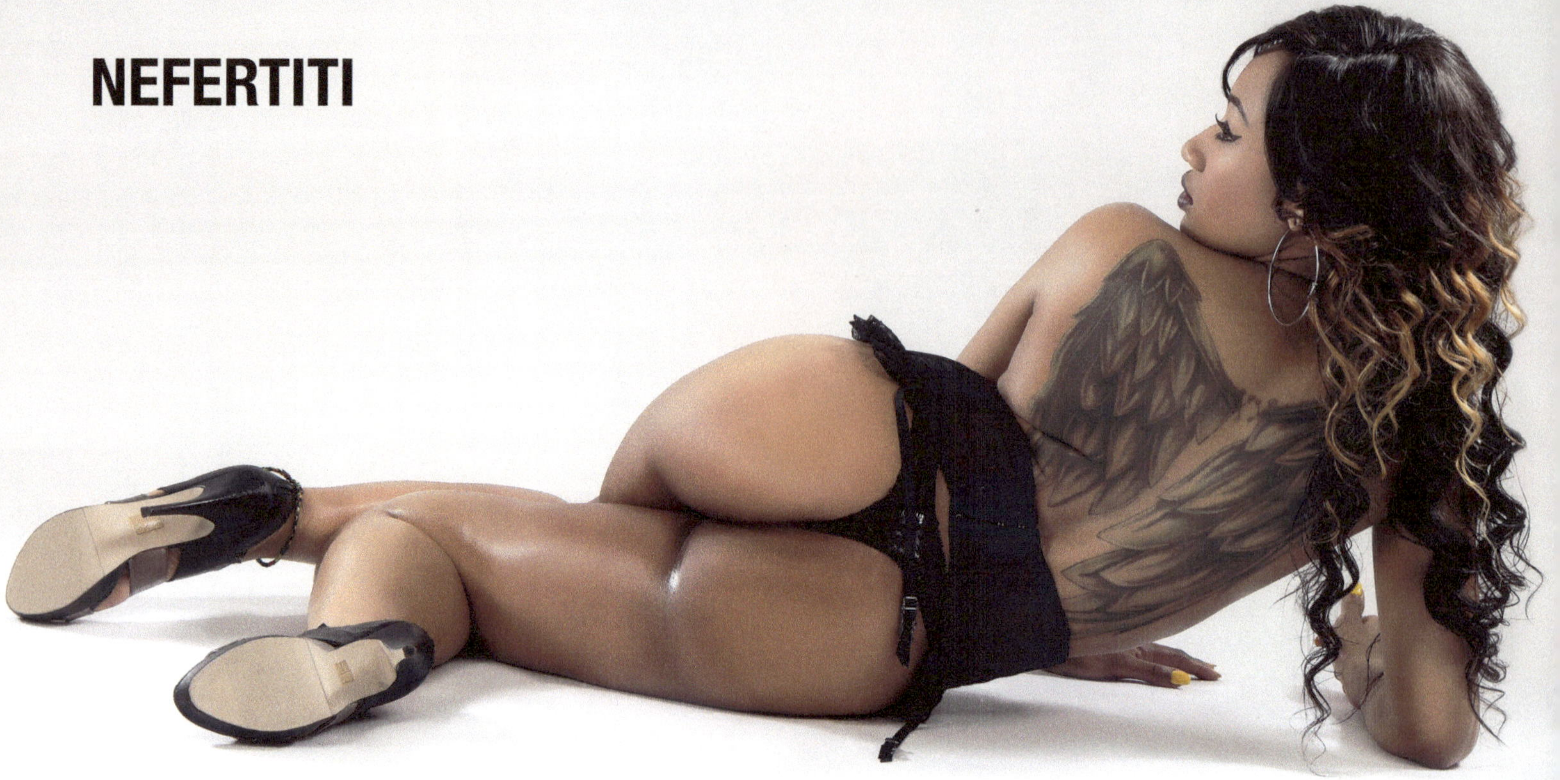

Now, what would you like people to be attracted to? *I would like people to be attracted to how smart I really am, and how good of a person I am.* **What is your Fetish?** *Cologne, I love when a guy smells good. It's intoxicating I swear.* **If a guy doesn't have a lot of money, he'd better have...** *ambition and drive to go get it. I mean, he doesn't have to be rich, but he will not mooch off of my dollars.* **Have you ever had a one night stand? Details?** *I have never had a one night stand, sorry ya girl just not breaking.* **What is the sexiest article of clothing you own?** *I would say leg wrap-arounds that strippers wear as their outfit, but i wear them as a GO Go dancer.* **If you had to sleep with a woman, who would be and how would you get her in bed?** *I would sleep with one of my Vine followers' girlfriend because she is just beautful [haha], no homo! I would just spit game to her... Ya know, like let her know I'm interested, and I'm sure she would be too.* **What do you normally sleep in?** *Nothing... Haha, studies say you should let it breathe at night, everything.*

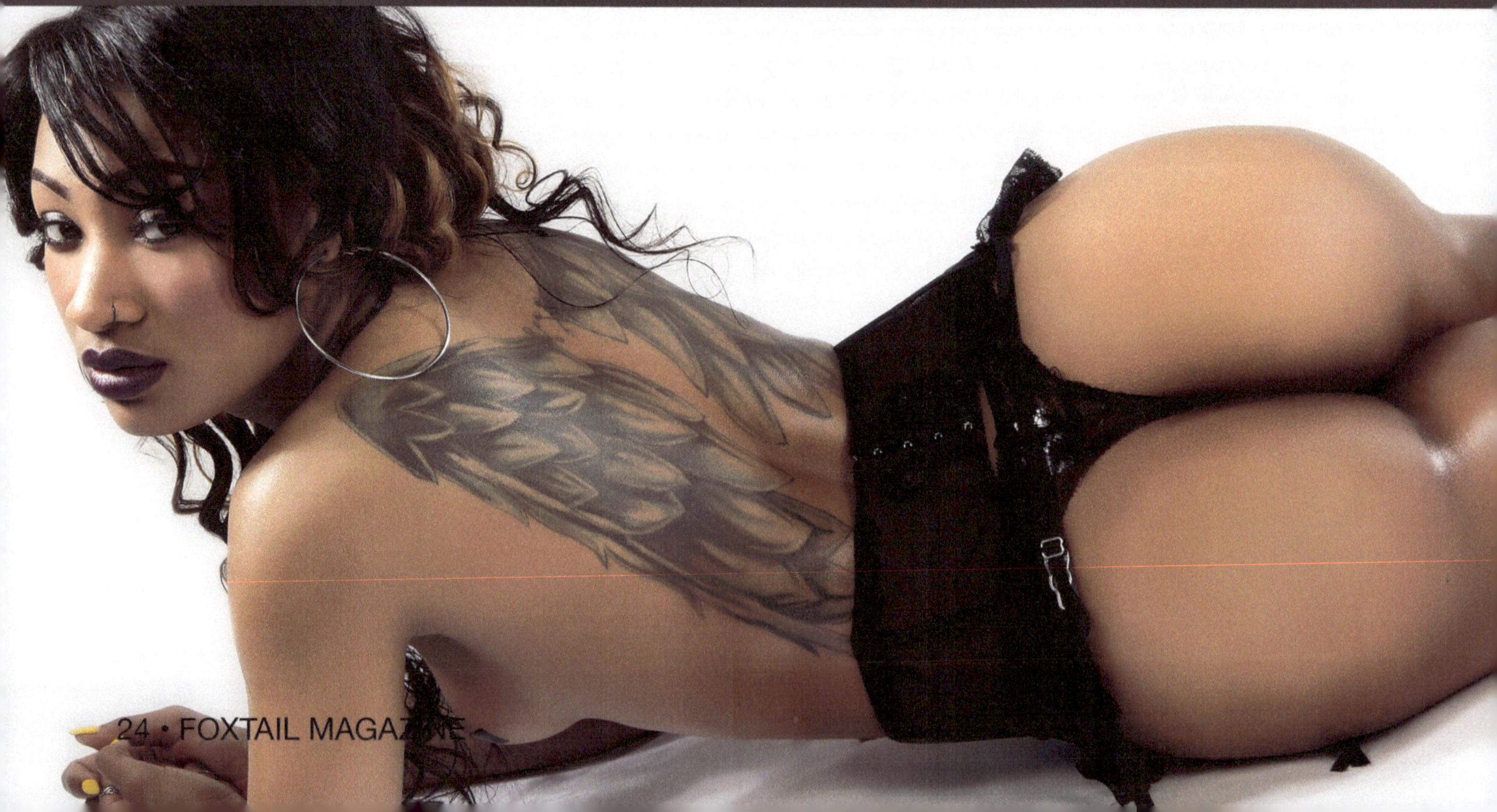

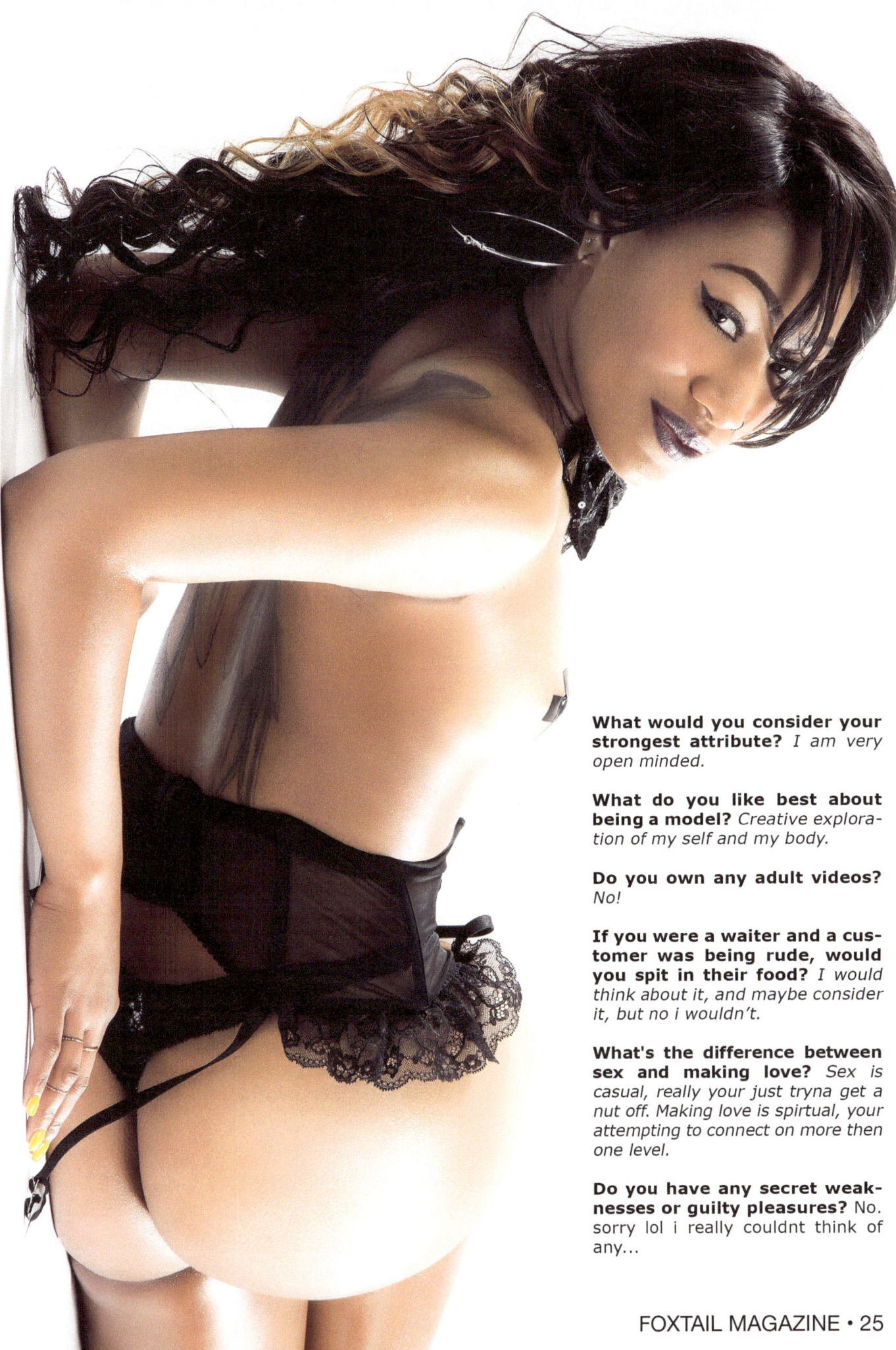

What would you consider your strongest attribute? *I am very open minded.*

What do you like best about being a model? *Creative exploration of my self and my body.*

Do you own any adult videos? *No!*

If you were a waiter and a customer was being rude, would you spit in their food? *I would think about it, and maybe consider it, but no i wouldn't.*

What's the difference between sex and making love? *Sex is casual, really your just tryna get a nut off. Making love is spirtual, your attempting to connect on more then one level.*

Do you have any secret weaknesses or guilty pleasures? *No. sorry lol i really couldnt think of any...*

COKAINA

PHOTOGRAPHY BY SINOVAH KANE

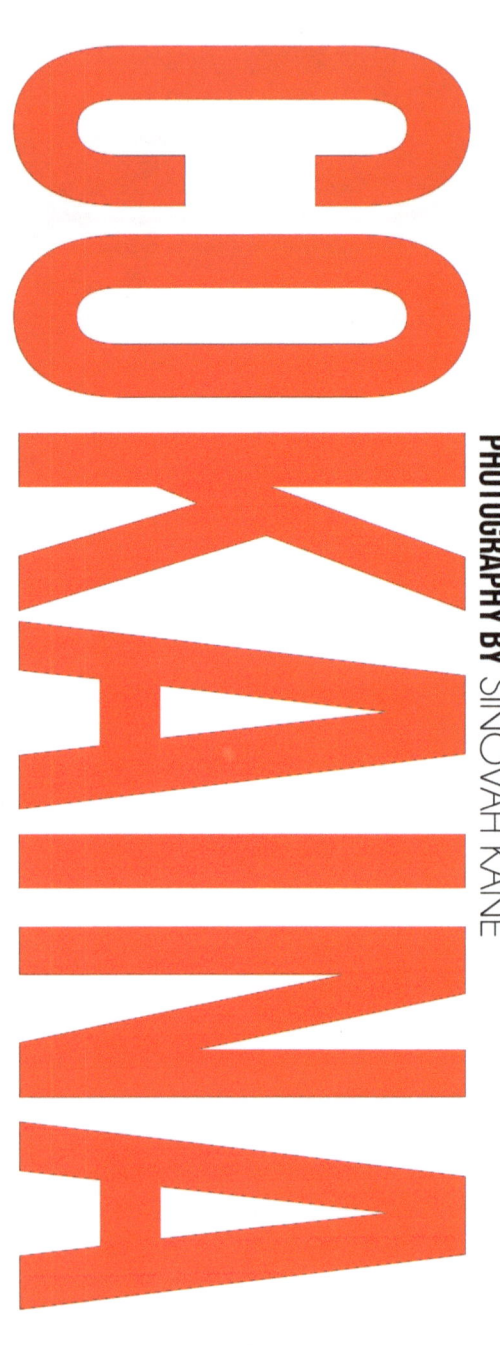

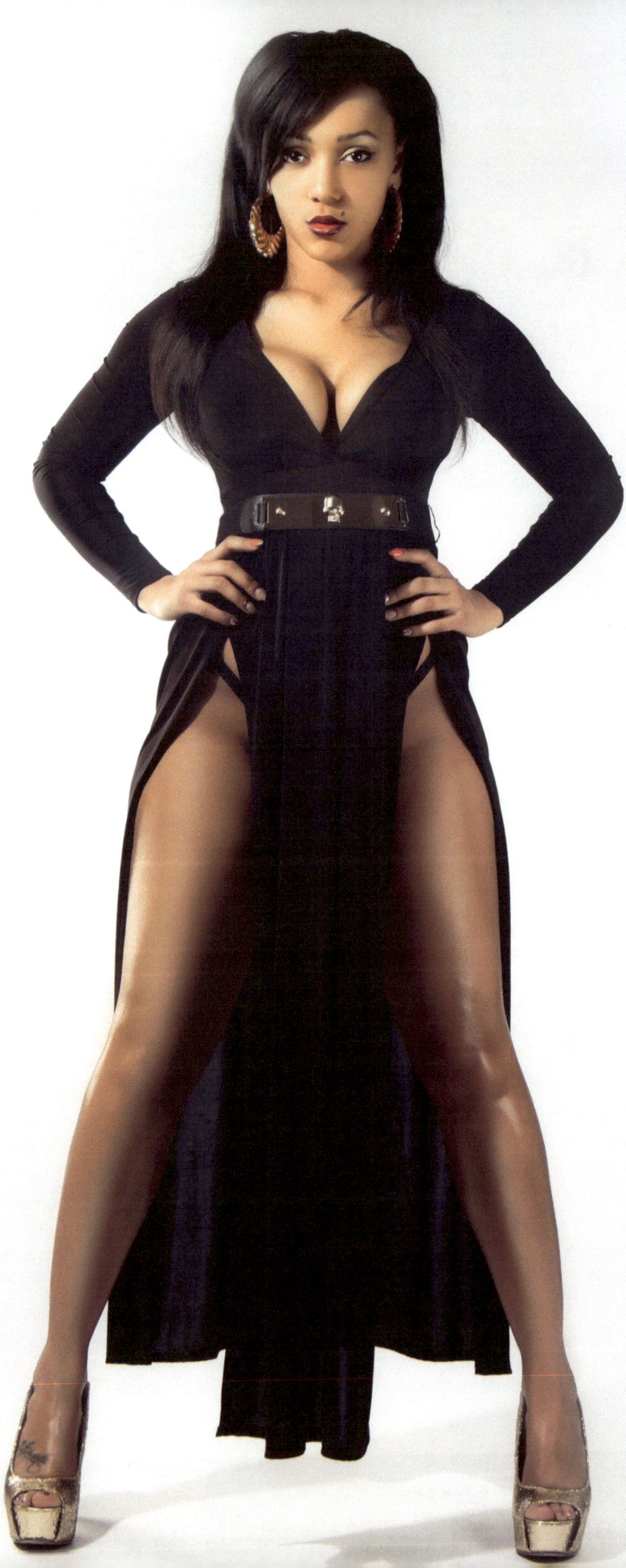

Age • 25
Nationality • Puerto Rican
Place of Birth • Indiana
Where do you rep? • Chicago

Height • 5'6
Weight • 135

Website • iCokaina.com
Twitter • iCokaina
Facebook • /CokaBaby

Profession • Entertainment

Relationship Status • The game was winning, So I married her!

Measurements • 34D- 26 - 40

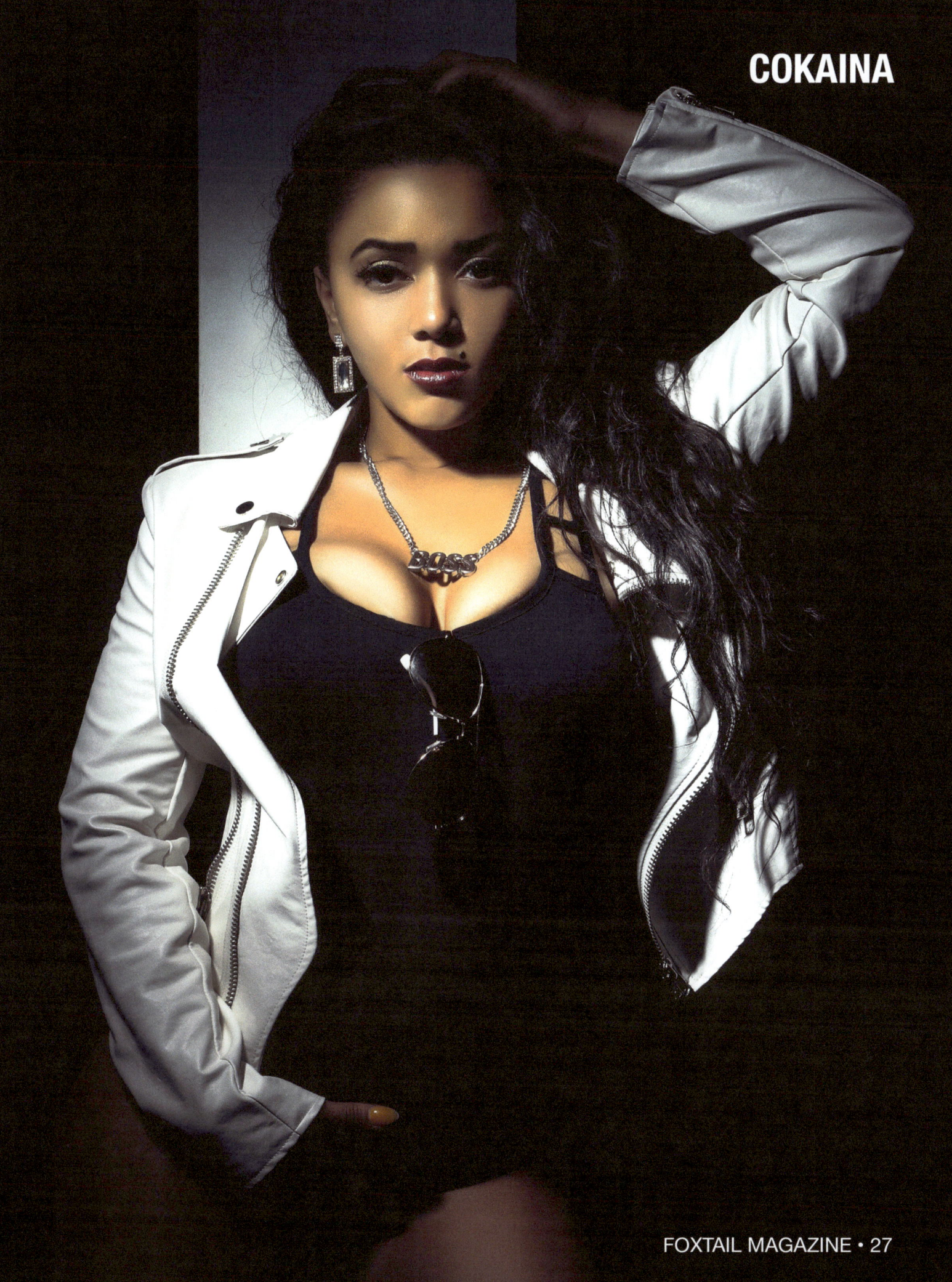

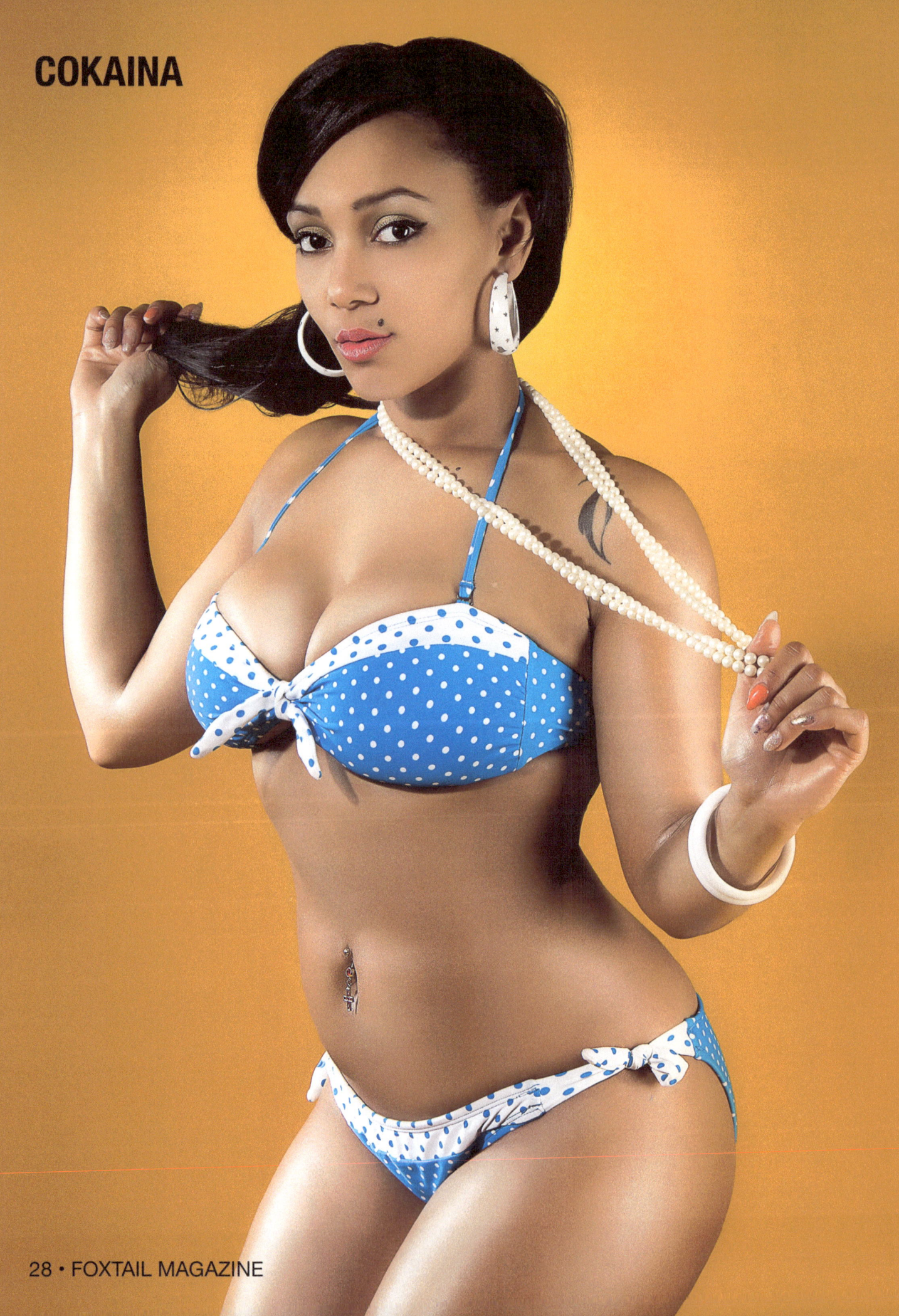

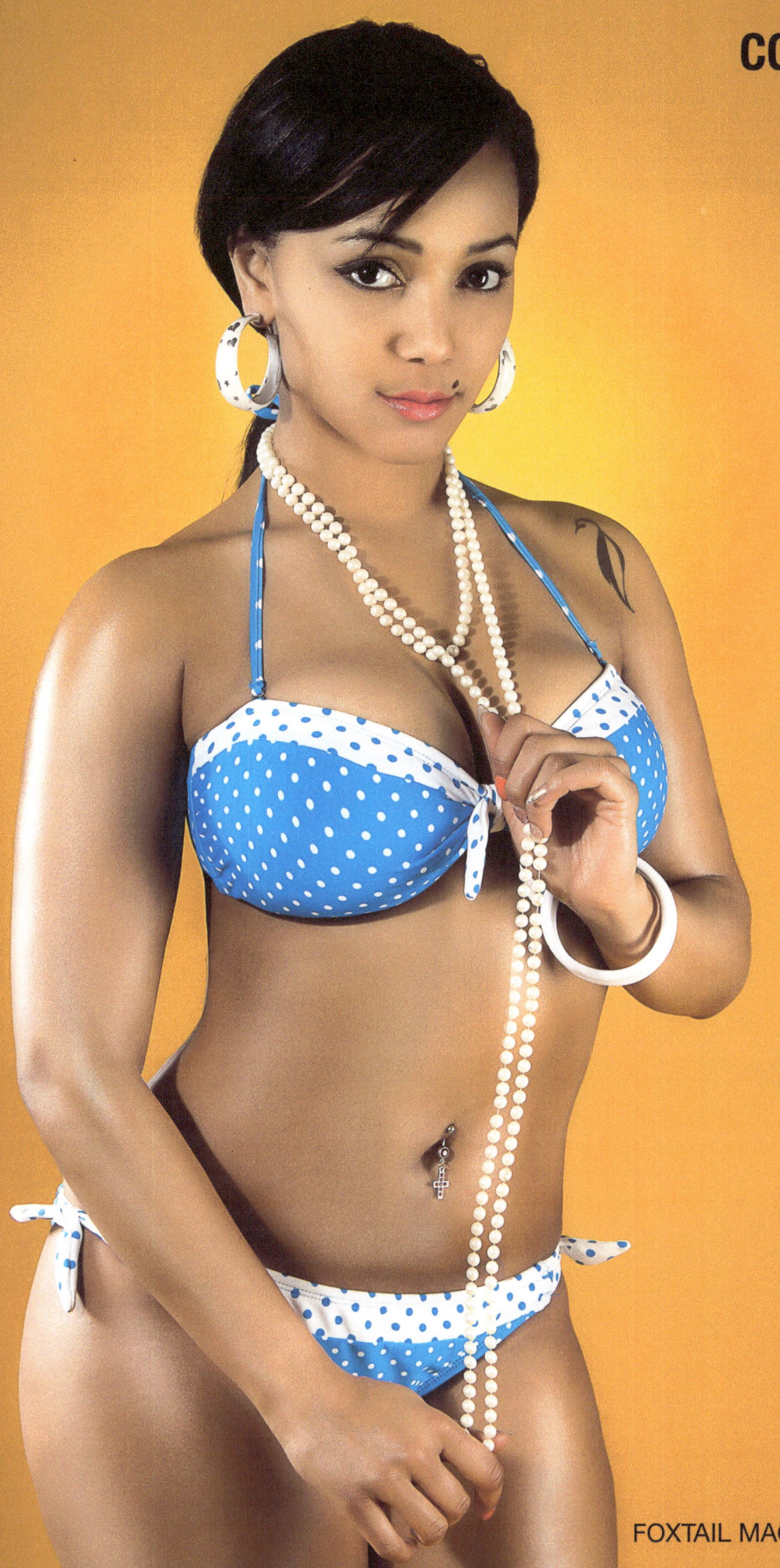

COKAINA

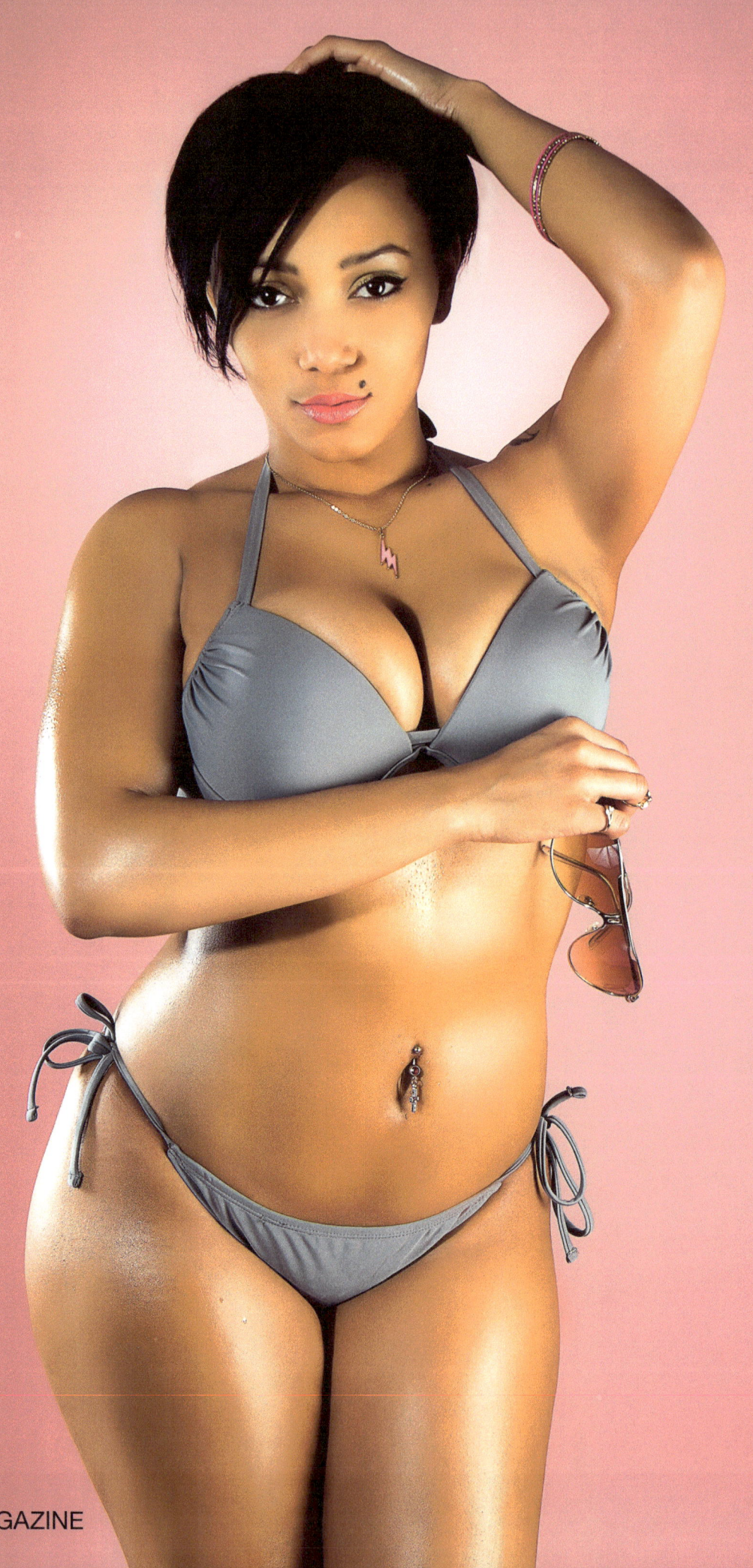

COKAINA

What's the worst lie you ever told? *I Love You!*

Did you get caught? *Nah!*

Would you rather be smart and ugly or dumb and beautiful? *Dumb and beautiful. Sorry, people don't like ugly people. Too much? You'll be okay.*

If you could be invisible, where would you go and what would you do? *I would follow around all the people I don't care for (like my boss) and splash water on them all day. Occasionally drop stuff right near them. Basically make them go crazy. Why not?*

Do you consider yourself more of a "giver" or a "taker"? *A giver. I may seem mean, at times, but I actually have a huge heart. I'll give u my last if u mean something to me.*

What's your biggest turn on? *A Smile.*

What would the average person say about you? *I'm feisty, but they love it.*

What do guys compliment you most on? *My eyes and smile. Don't know why my eyes because they're plain ol' brown, but I'll take it.*

What is your Fetish? *The V.*

If you don't have a lot of money, you better have... *A great personality. Broke and annoying is not cute.*

Ever had a one night stand? Details? *I have. Common, really? We smashed and I never called him again. ¯_(ツ)_/¯*

Now, what would you like people to be attracted to? *My face, more so, than my ass and/or tithes.*

What is the sexiest article of clothing you own? *My skin.*

If you had to sleep with someone of the same, who would be and how would you get them in bed? *Rihanna. I would spark up a blunt next to her. Mission accomplished.*

Tell us a funny, but dirty joke... *How are women and tornadoes alike? They both moan like hell when they come, and take the house when they leave.*

What would you consider your strongest attribute? *Follow me and choose for yourself. That's how we can play that game.*

What's your biggest turn on? *Being a realist and confidence!*

What do you like best about being a model? *Taking pretty pictures!*

Do you own any adult videos? *Nah, I use PornHub!*

If you were a waiter and a customer was being rude, would you spit in their food? *I am a server in real life and I don't spit in people's food. But, I do wish them a horrible day and kick rock son!*

What's the difference between sex and making love? *A lot. Too much to explain. Most people will never understand.*

THE REAL LAX

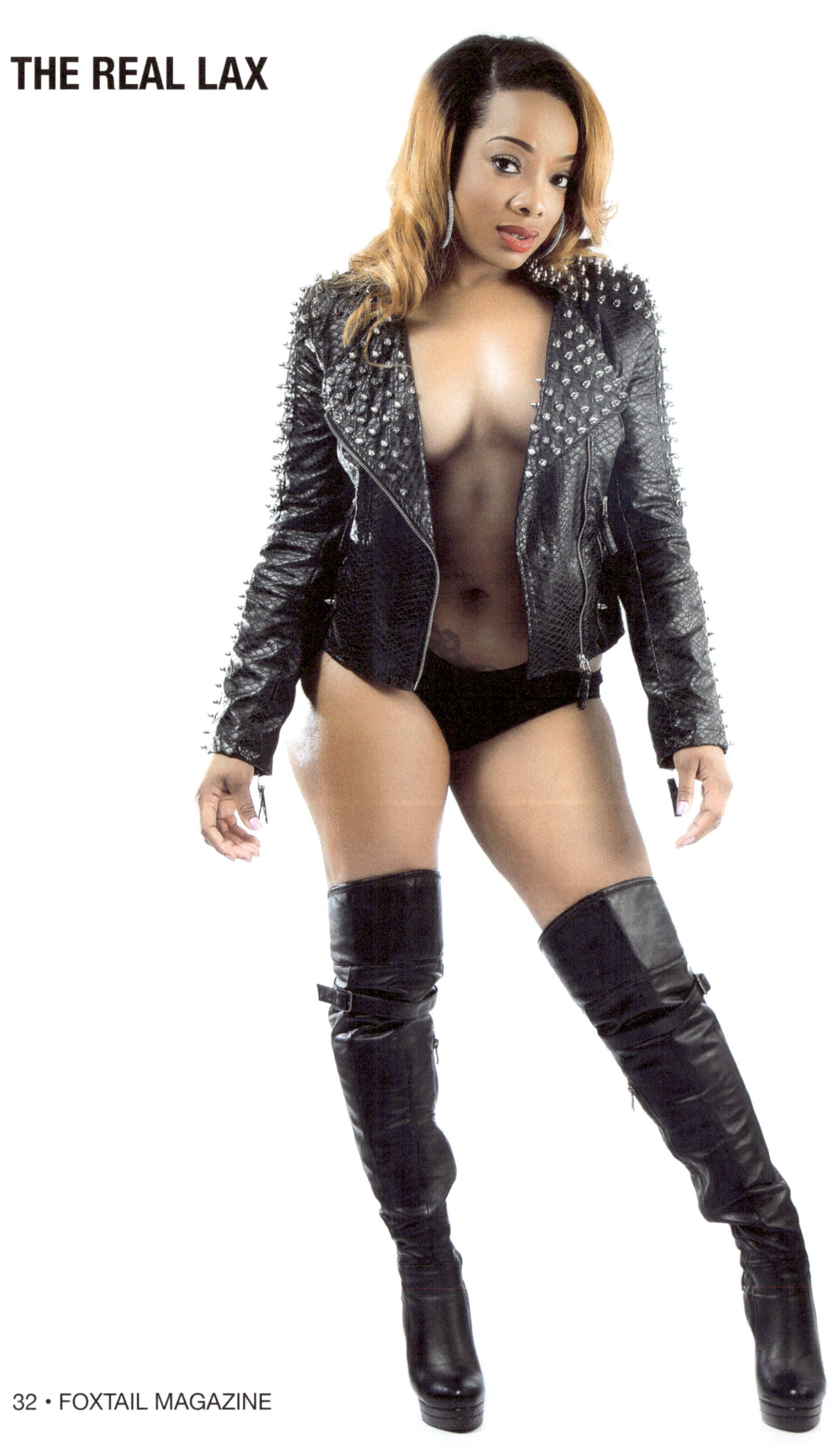

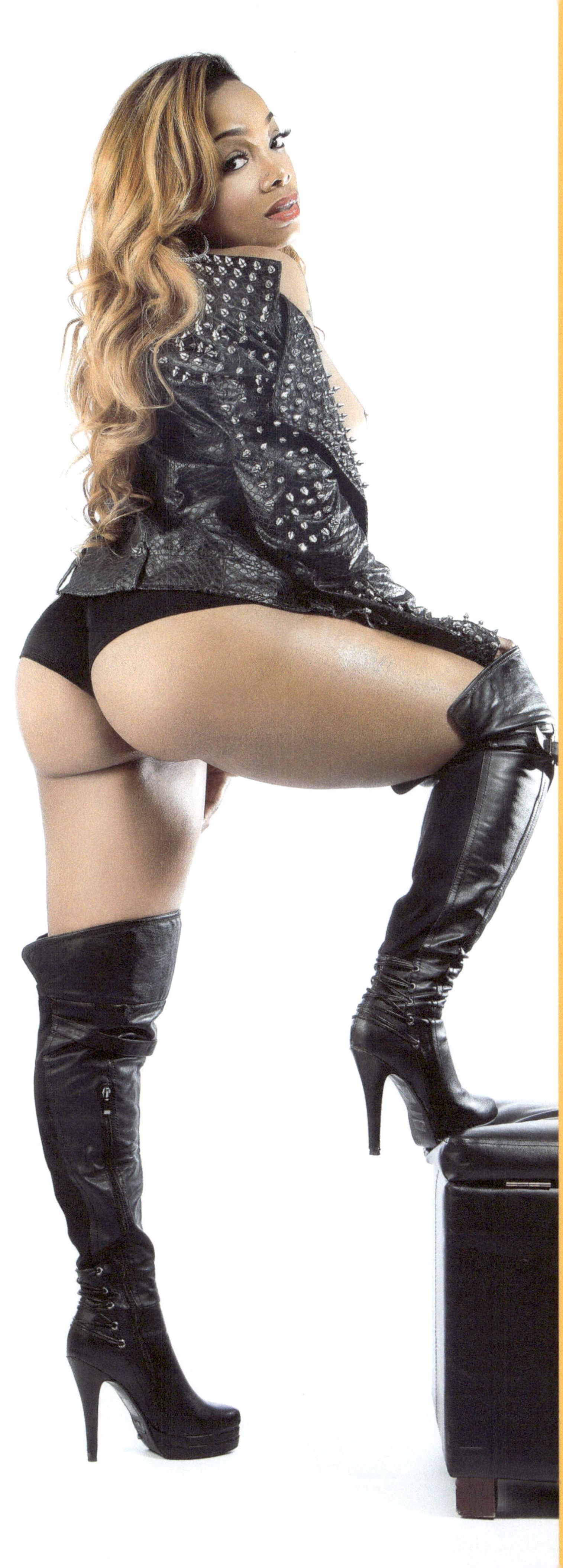

THE REAL LAX

PHOTOGRAPHY BY SINOVAH KANE

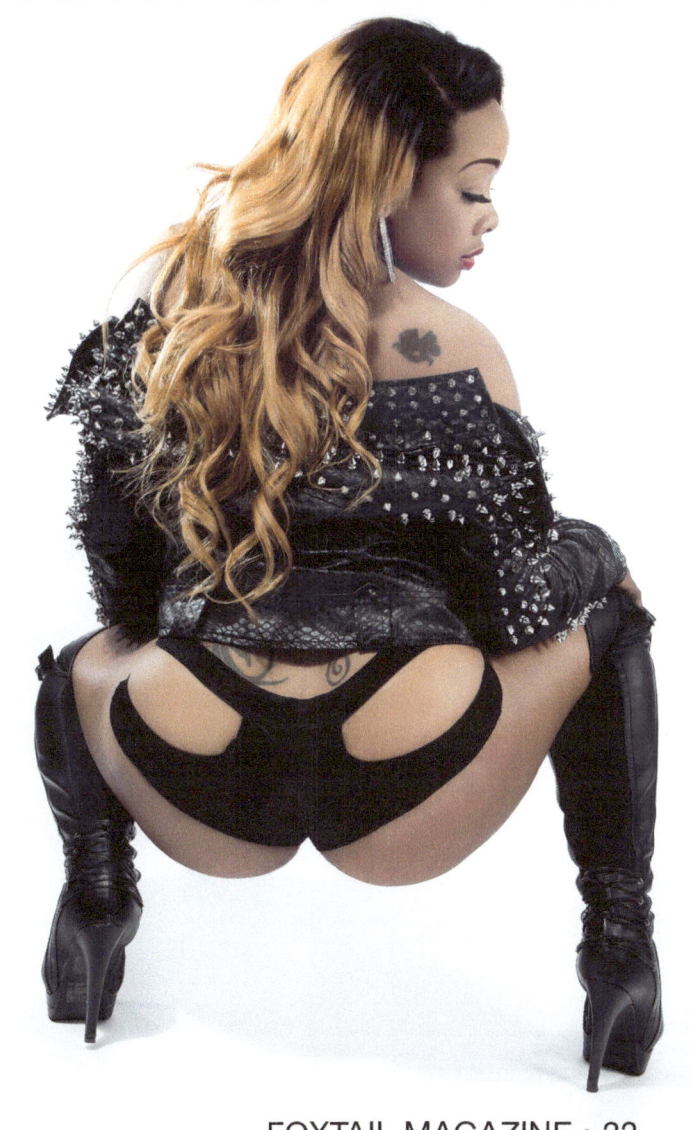

FOXTAIL MAGAZINE • 33

THE REAL LAX

34 • FOXTAIL MAGAZINE

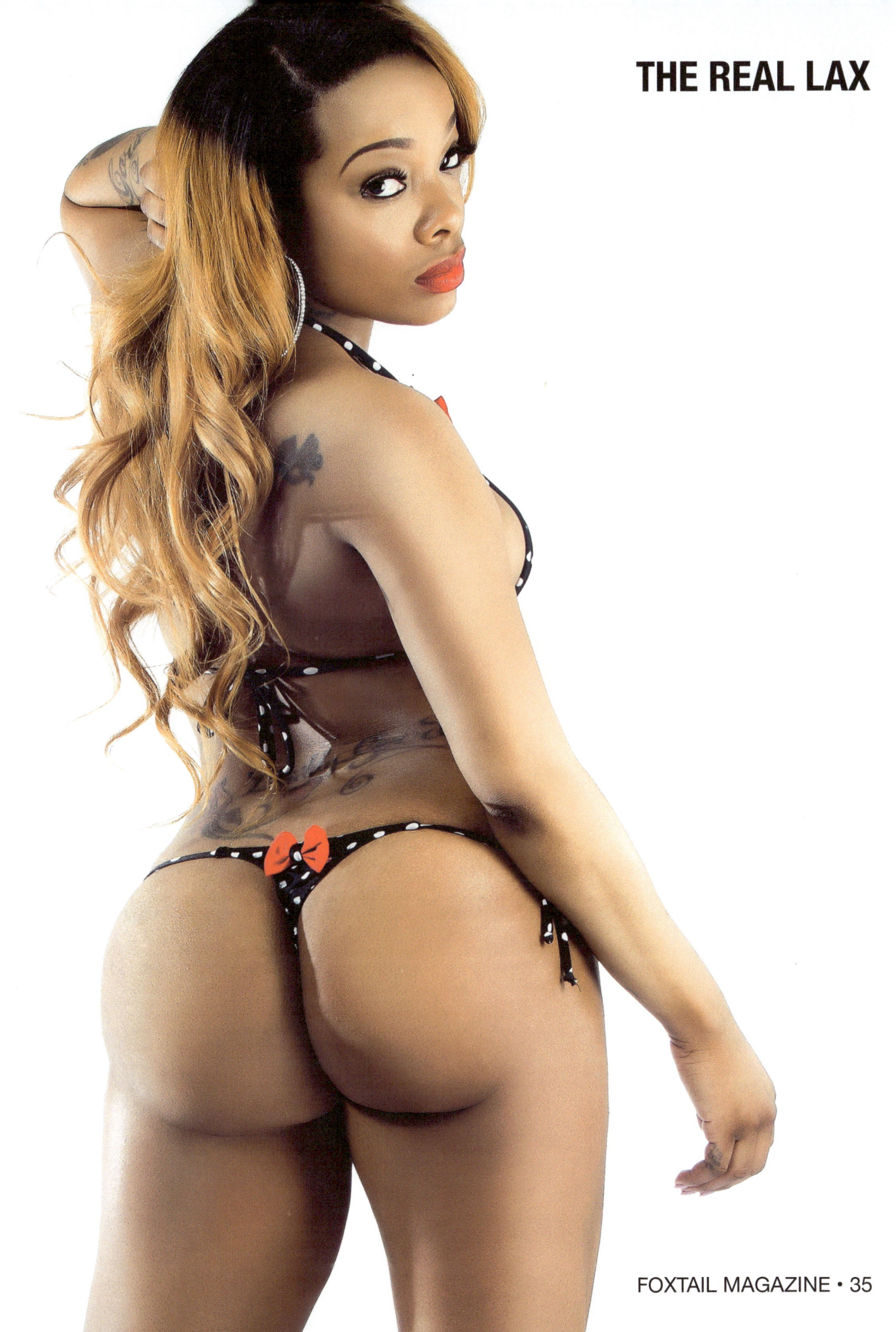

THE REAL LAX

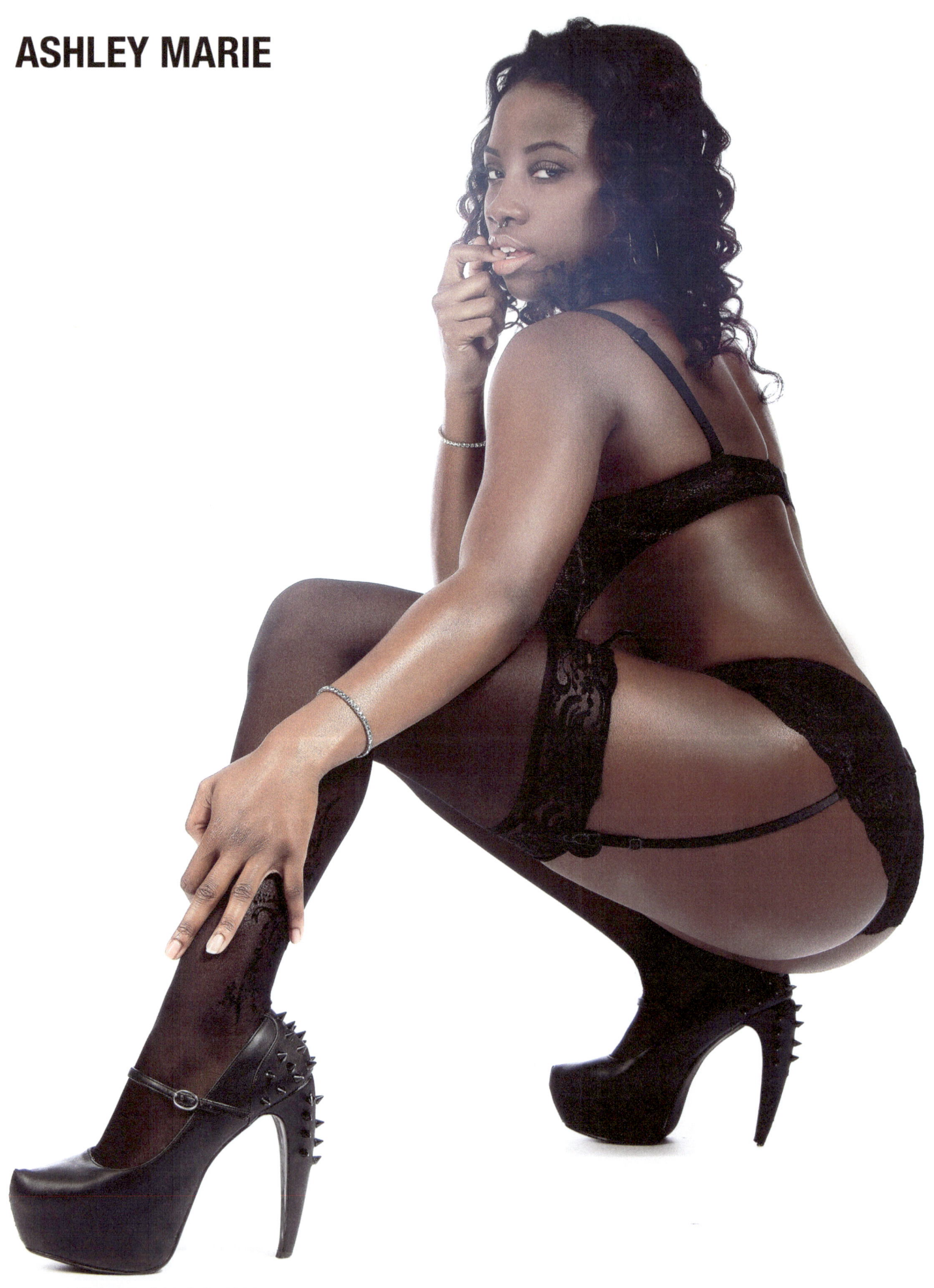

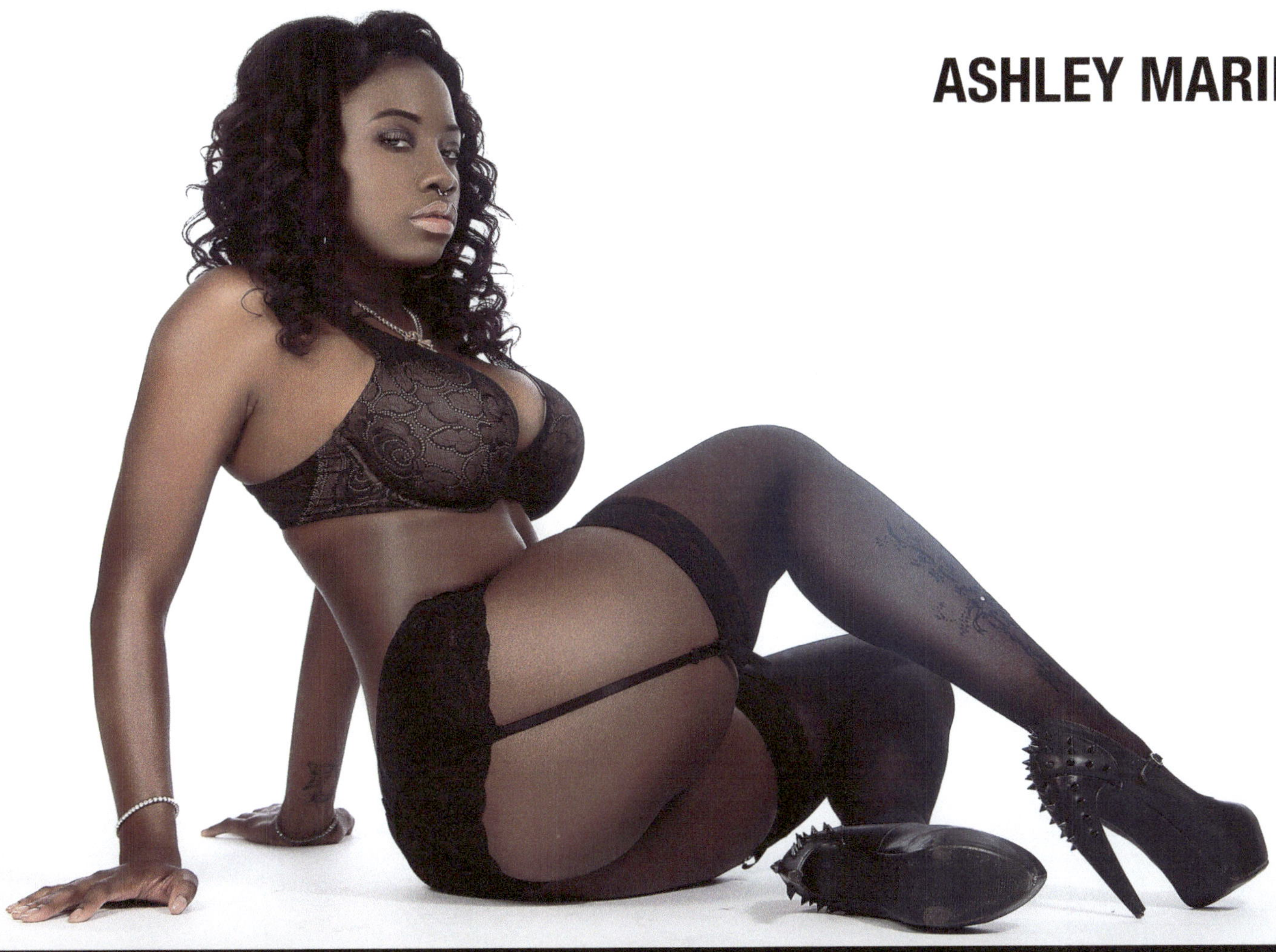

ASHLEY MARIE

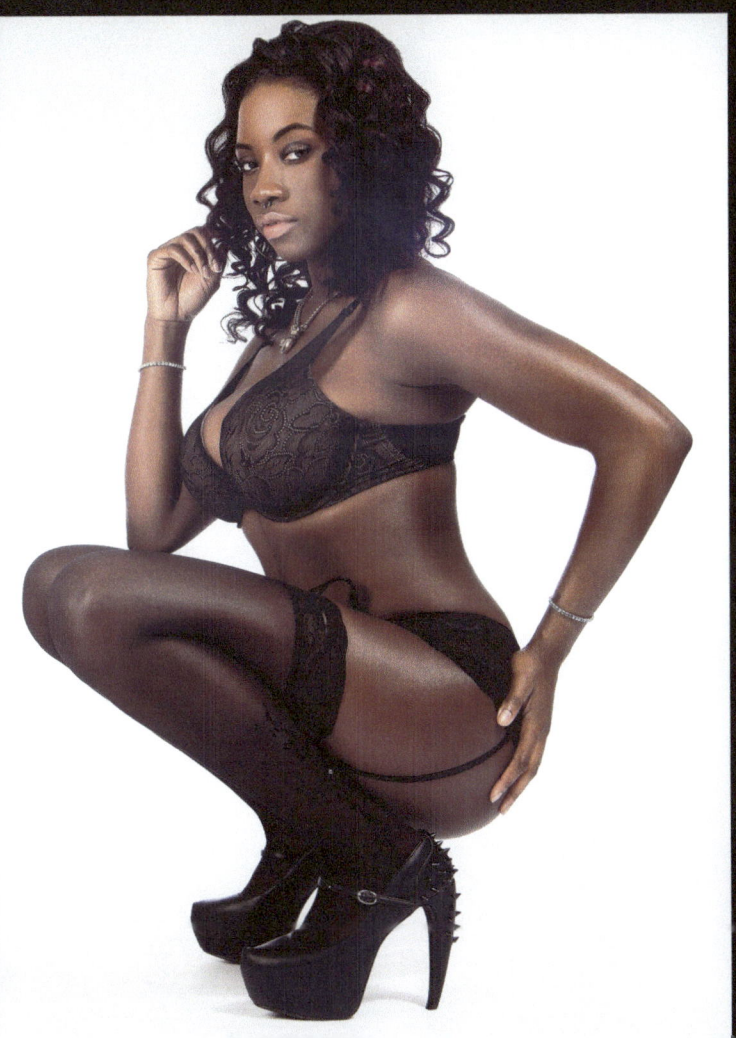

ASHLEY MARIE

PHOTOGRAPHY BY SINOVAH KANE

AGE • 21 **NATIONALITY** • African American **PLACE OF BIRTH** • Chicago, IL **HEIGHT** • 5' 8" **WEIGHT** • 160 lbs. **TWITTER** • _gorgeousash_ **WEBSITE** • Modelmayhem.com/2176693 **PROFESSION** • Model / Bartender / College Student **RELATIONSHIP STAUTS** • Single **MEASUREMENTS** • 36-28-40

ASHLEY MARIE

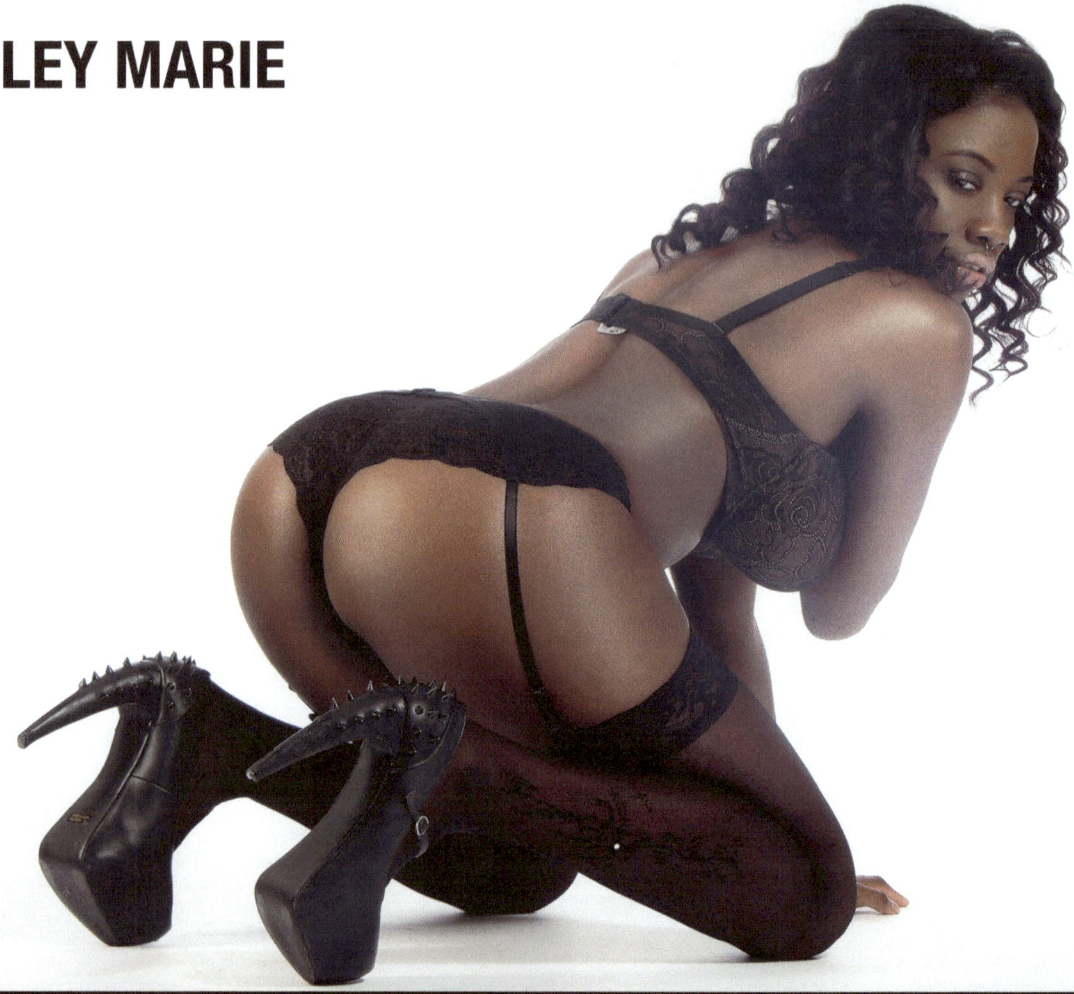

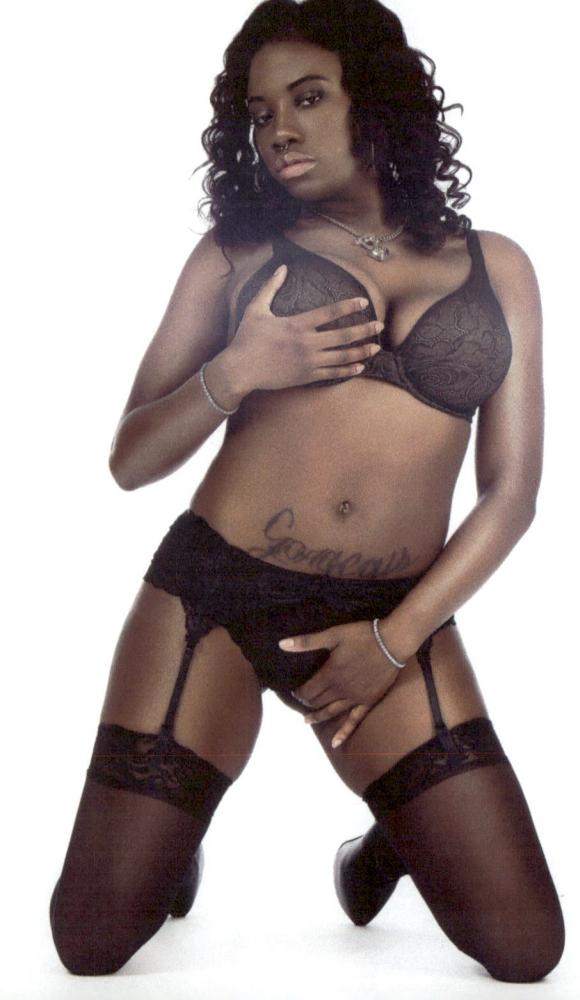

ALL ABOUT ME!

Would you rather be smart and ugly, or dumb and beautiful? *I would rather be smart and ugly only because beauty can only get you so far if you don't have the right personality.*

If you could be invisible, where would you go and what would you do? *I would go to a few banks and take all their cash from the safes.lol*

Do you consider yourself more of a "giver" or a "taker"? *It depends on who the person. If it's someone I care about, then I'm a giver. I would do anything to make sure my love ones are good.*

What would the average person say about you? *That I am a nice person, and I'm gorgeous :)*

What do guys compliment you most on? *My smile and body.* **Now, what would you like people to be attracted to?** *My personality first.*

What is your Fetish? *Biting.*

If a guy doesn't have a lot of money, he'd better have… *a plan working towards some type of goals that will get him some money.*

38 • FOXTAIL MAGAZINE

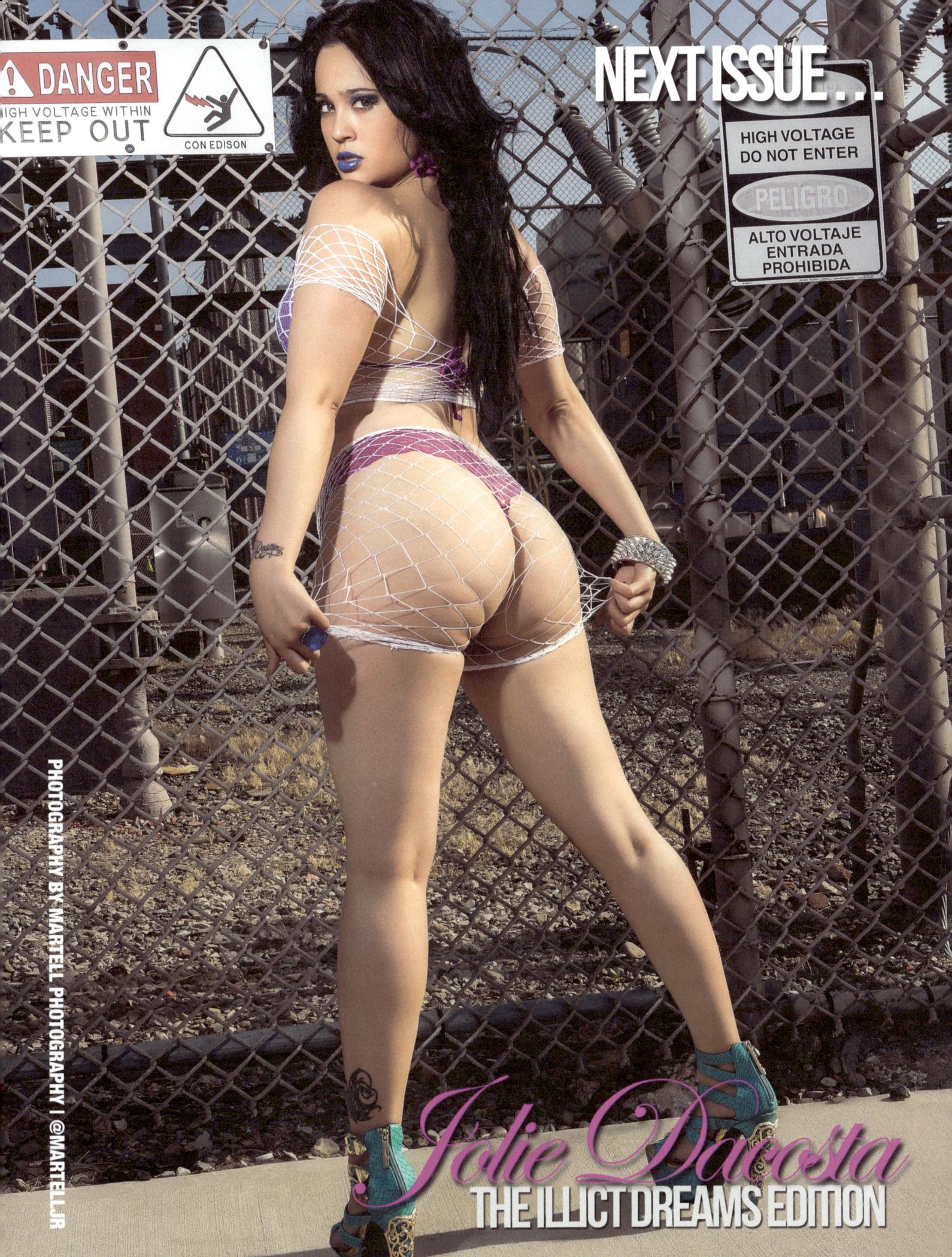

THE MAN CAVE *AND STUFF EVERY CAVE NEEDS*

Every man should have mancave. In that cave, one must have "only" the most super cool man toys ever built. The man toys must be so cool, they literally make other men whimper with envy. Your man cave must be so swagged out, that the only appropriate acknowledgement one can receive is, "Dude, You are the Man!" So here are a few toys we have in our man cave! Enjoy! Do you have somethig for the man cave, email us at mancave@foxtailmag.com

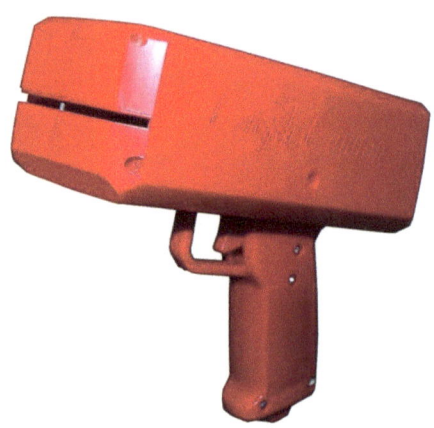

MAKE IT RAIN CASH CANNON - *$59.99*

By now, I'm sure we've all heard the term, "Makin It Rain"! Well, with this nifty little device, you won't just make it rain; you will be causing a monsoon all over your favorite stripper in no time. The Cash Cannon is a novelty product that enables you to literally fire single dollar bills into the air like a hail of bullets. Just whip little boy out at your next Vegas strip club bachelor party, and I guarantee you will be surrounded by more body glitter, G-strings and bouncing tittes than you'll know what to do with.

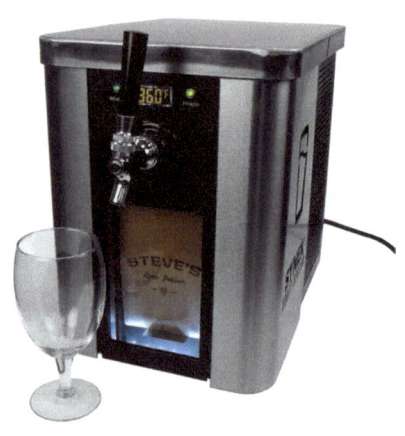

SYNEK COUNTERTOP DRAFT BEER SYSTEM - *$59.99*

Do you ever get tired of going to the local pub for a pint? Have you ever wished for the great taste of on-tap draft beer, right, in the comfort of your own home? Well, the boys down at SYNEK are working on making your wildest dreams come true. SYNEK has created a countertop draft system that sure to revolutionize the home draft beer industry. Their system guarantees fresh beer from any tap while preserving the beer's original taste and quality with their patent pending SYNEK bags. This countertop draft beer system guaranteed all the best qualities of your local pub right at home with that smell of stale beer and cigarettes.

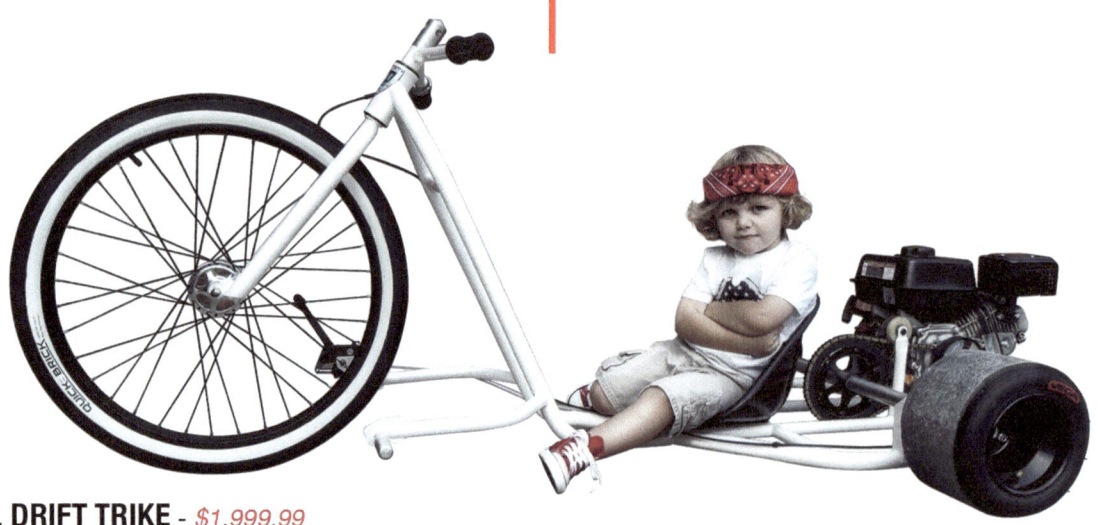

BIG WHEEL DRIFT TRIKE - *$1,999.99*

Okay. Let's put things in perspective. Now why would a grown man spend two thousand dollars on an over-sized big wheel? Well, because… it has an engine. Duh! I thought that was clear already! Furthermore, I had the biggest, baddest big wheel on the block when I was a child, and it clear nothing has changed! Thank to the genius of August Agner of SFD Industries, Agner and his team manufacture the only motorized drift trike on the planet. Each trike's chassis is CNC bent out of .095 chrome, and tig welded and assembled in house. The standard, base level big wheel features include: rear brakes, buyer's choice of standard powder coat, black anodized rims, Big-rig 26" X 3" front wheel, twist throttle, and a whooping 6.5hp motor. Yeah, wait until the neighborhood gets a load of me!

THE WHEELS

Ferrari's LaFerrari

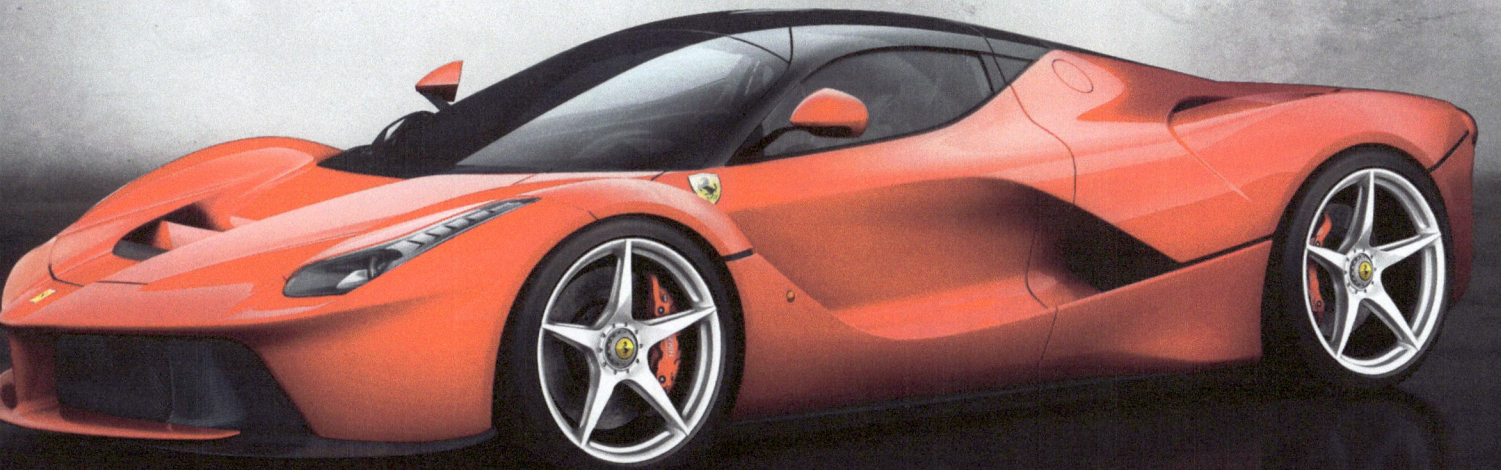

"We call it Laferrari because it is the maximum expression of what defines our company – Excellence." - Luca di Montezemolo

THE SPECS

HORSEPOWER	950
TORQUE	660
TOP SPEED	218
0-60 MPH	< 3.0S
0-186 MPH	< 15.0S
ENGINE CYL/ DISPLACEMENT	V-12/ 6.3L
PRODUCTION QUANTITY	499
PRICE	$1,400,000

If you ask your favorite celebrity rapper, then a Bugatti Vernon would probably be your car of choice when it comes to high-end, exorbitantly priced, super sport cars. However, if your anything like me, and burdened with the unfortunate aliment of thinking for oneself, then you probably have your own choice of super cars. Personally, I prefer the classics. Nothing is more of a classic, than the Ferrari.

The Ferrari, La Ferrari, marks the succession of the legendary Ferrari Enzo. The biggest shocker was the name. According to President Luca di Montezemolo, when asked about the name, the name was chosen, "because it is the maximum expression of what defines our company – excellence."

The LaFerrari is designed to be the prefect combination of form and function. The model uses F1-inspired aerodynamics. Just like the exterior, the company's track cars inspire the interior. Everything is tailored to the driver, and both the pedal box and steering where are adjustable. Let's face it, despite the unusual name, the LaFerrari isn't a bad way to spend 1.4 million dollars.

THE LOOK BOOK

THE FRESHMAN

It's not your first rodeo, but it just might be your first day. You don't know anyone, so you're very eager to impress everyone. You want people to notice you. Well, you can certainly do that with the "Lil Ben" by Sprayground.

THE "LIL BEN"
by Sprayground
$60.00

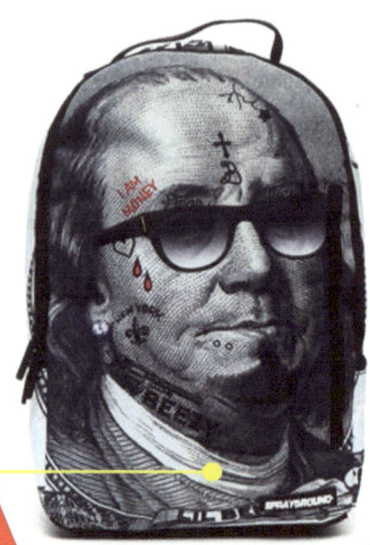

THE JUNIOR

You have finally reached that pivotal moment we all reach when we realized that we are young enough to do it, but old enough to know better. Validation from others is no longer of any interest to you, but looking good is still of the utmost concern to you. You like to keep it appealing but keep it simple. You go for the classics like those from North Face.

THE "CREVASSE"
by NorthFace
$99.00

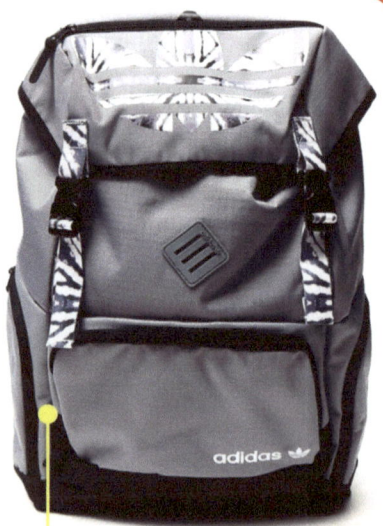

THE BACK PACKER

I know what you're thinking. Backpacks aren't your typical fashion trend. Truth of the matter is backpacks aren't just for high schoolers. Many adults choose backpacks over the usual briefcase or carrying bag. Nonetheless, choosing a backpack over a briefcase on your way anywhere says a lot about you. So, we've selected a few of this year's hottest backpacks, and we are going to tell you what your backpack says about you!

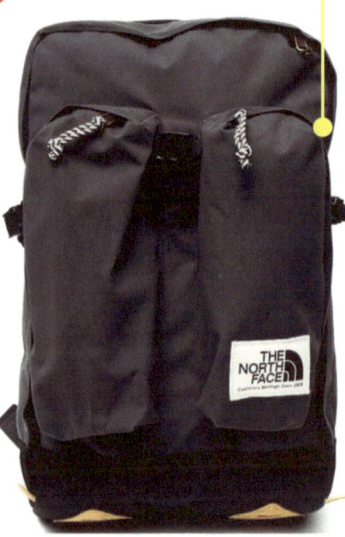

THE SOPHOMORE

It's clear you have been around the block once or twice. You know the neighbors and all the shortcuts to getting around. You're not looking so much for validation, but you still definitely want to dress to impress. Well, Addidas has just the bag for you.

THE "COMTEMPORARY"
by ADDIAS
$65.00

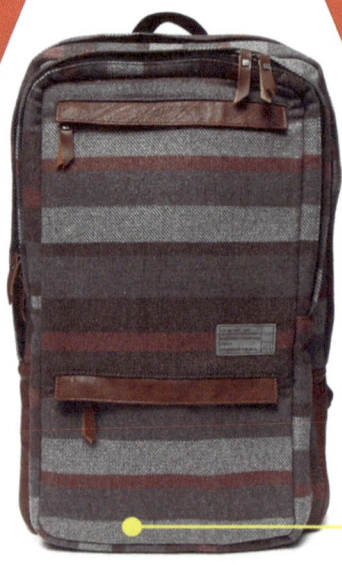

THE SENIOR

You have finally arrived! You are the master of your destiny. You know exactly who you are and what you want to be in life. You have absolutely no need for validation. You don't just to dress to impress, you dress for success. You look good. You smell good. You feel good. It's a man's world. You can be fashion conscious without being taken the wrong way. Yeah, this backpack by Hex has it all.

THE "SONIC WESTMORE"
by Hex
$99.99

42 • FOXTAIL MAGAZINE

SHOE PORN | *The Best Things in Life Come in Pairs*

Be Prepared for Every Occassion

When it comes to footwear, you should never be the guy without options. Show up to a nightclub in the same scuffed Air Force Ones you wore all day, and you won't have to speculate why you're still standing in line outside of the club. Having two feet doesn't mean you only need two shoes.

FOR WORK

When it comes to climbing the corporate ladder, nothing puts the finishing touches on your dress ensemble with undeniable appeal like the Ponte Monk Strap by Salvatore Ferragamo.

Salvatore Feggagamo Ponte Monk Strap
$740.00

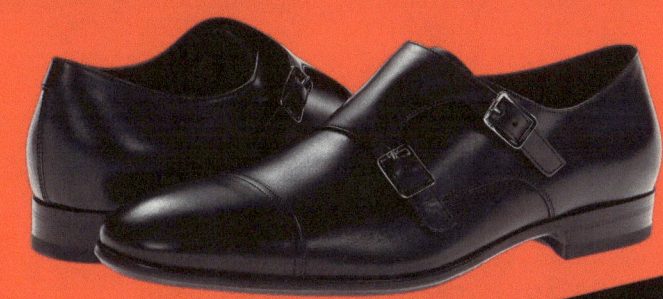

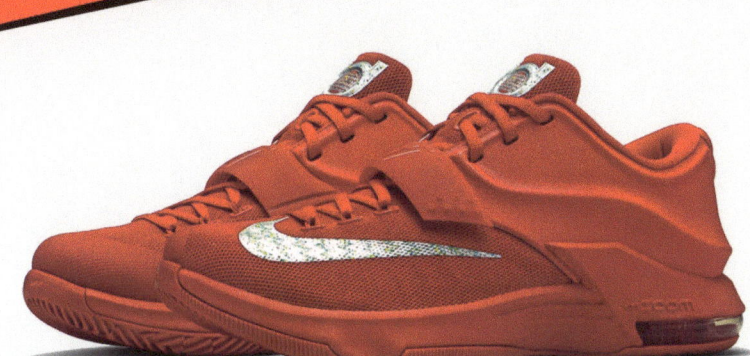

FOR PLAY

These bad boys were created by Nike designer Leo Chang. They meets Durant's need for quickness, power and unpredictability, just like the forces of nature. Now your turn!

Nike KD7 'Global Game'
$150.00

FOR AFTER HOURS

When you finally get that one night stand home, you probably want to be as comfortable as possible. Nothing say comfort like a pair sheepskin slippers.

UGG Ascot
$110.00

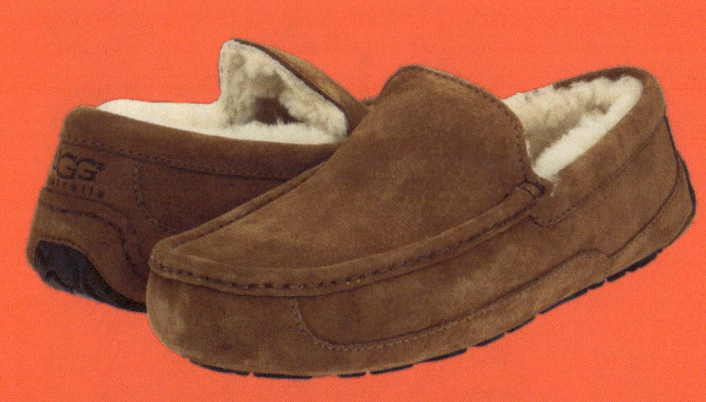

DATING GAME

DON'T BE THAT GUY, GUY!

BY ANGIE V

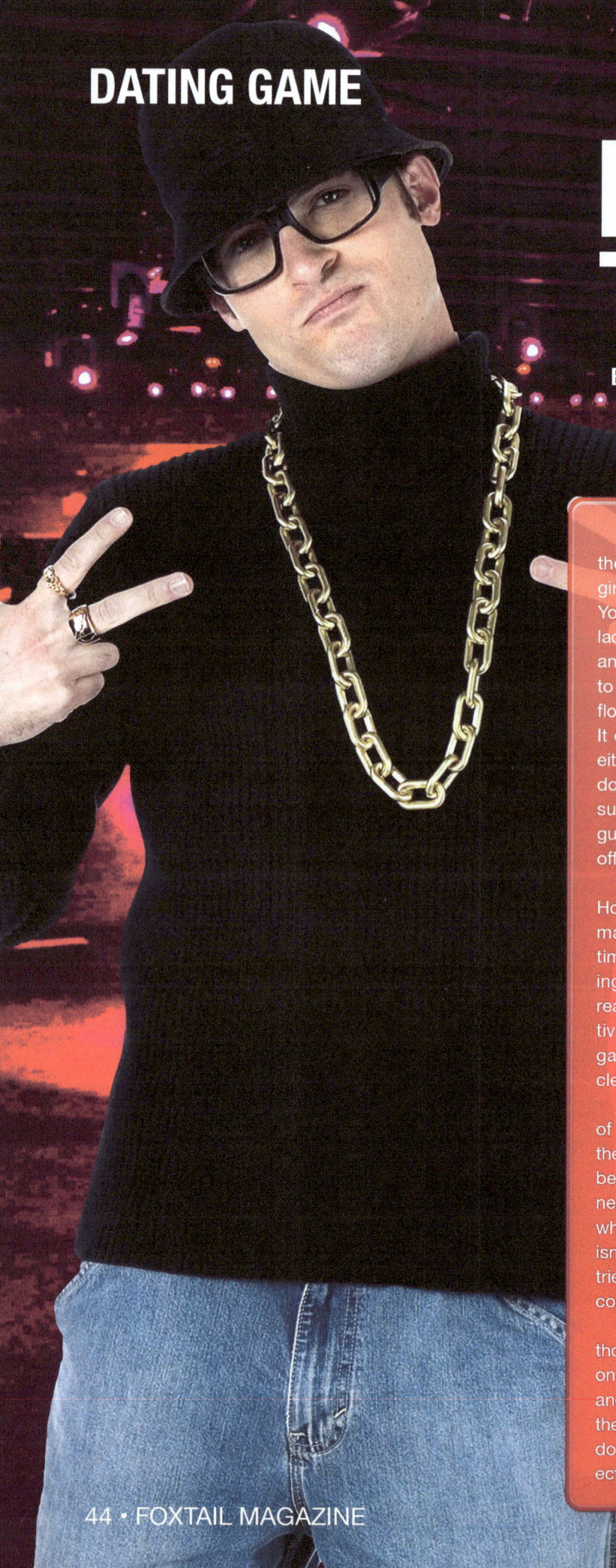

You know who I'm talking about. You see him on the train, the bus, the mall, at the supermarket. He's everywhere. 'Hey girl, where you going?', 'Can I come with you?', 'Damn, girl. You sexy.', 'Aye, ma! Aye!' He swears up and down he's a ladies man. He's not. Women go to great lengths to avoid his annoying ass, but to no avail. Whether he's desperately trying to buy a girl a drink or awkwardly staring across the dance floor trying to make eye contact; This. Guy. Is. EVERYWHERE. It doesn't help that he has rejection issues most of the time either. Seemingly sweet and harmless, but once you let him down gently (or not), that's usually when shit hits the fan. Insults start flying, you end up being verbally berated and this guy ends up with a bruised ego. For the sake of your future offspring, don't be that guy.

If a female is interested, chances are, you'll be able to tell. How? 2 words. Body Language. You'll notice she possibly may have shifted, her body is now facing you a bit more. At times, you'll notice obviously stolen glances. She'll be fidgeting with her hair. Pretending to look in your direction (she's really just checking you out on the low.) You have to be attentive and notice little things like that. Make eye contact, (Don't gawk though. Awkward much?) smile sincerely, and make it clear you'd like to get to know her.

Engage in friendly conversation, break the ice with a sense of humor and casually ask if she'd like to get lunch 'one of these days'. Notice the emphasis around 'one of these days' because there will be no pressure to meet up, as next week or next month could be 'one of these days'. Granted, a woman who takes her sweet time to communicate with you probably isn't interested but you would have never known unless you tried. The thought of lunch with someone is also less pressure considering dinner usually follows up with a night cap.

Some welcome the dinner and night cap, but be weary of those who want a little less formality in getting to know someone. I mean, last thing you want is to go out to a fancy dinner and it be awkward. As. Hell. (Can you say 'Check please?') At the end of the day, just know it's not what you do, it's how you do it. You're already a smooth gentleman. Now you got to project that.

FEED ME THIS!

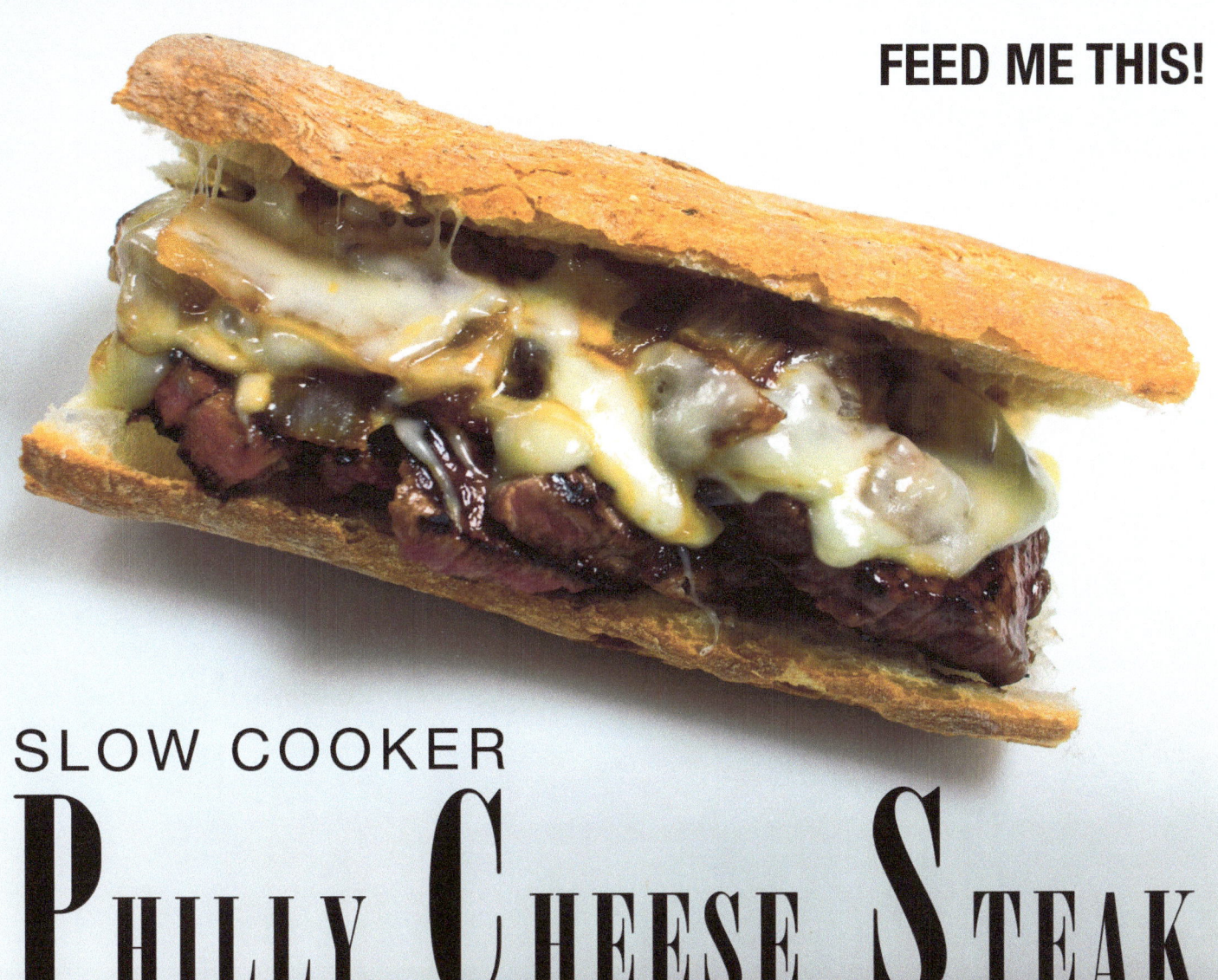

SLOW COOKER
Philly Cheese Steak

Over the years, Mom has given me some sound advice. Like don't take candy from strange men who hang out near children's playgrounds. Whatever you do... please, don't become the strange man handing out candy near the children's playgrounds. Always wear a condom. Yes, es-special-ly when she says she's on the pill! Last but not least, I was told to learn to cook for myself. If you'd have asked me, I wouldn't need cooking lessons due to the slew of beautiful Playboy models I would eventually have serving me breakfast in bed. Since Mom usually knew best, I decided to learn how to cook anyway, despite the super models. Thanks mom!

In honor of the wonderful advice of mothers everywhere, we will be learning to make "Slow Cooker Philly Cheese Steak". Philly steaks are the cornerstone of every man's meal. Why? Because they have meat in them! Men love meat! Especially, when that meat is on the backside of a young pole dancer. This time the meat is between a pair of buns (pun intended). Now, go grab your mother's Crock pot, and let's get cooking.

INGREDIENTS

- 1 1/2 lbs beef round steak
- 1 green pepper, sliced thin
- 1 medium onion, sliced thin
- 1 (14 oz) can beef broth
- 1 envelope Italian dressing mix
- 1 large loaf French bread, siced into sandwich lengths (or 4-6 hoagie buns)
- Provolone cheese slices

DIRECTIONS

1. Spray your crock pot with a non-stick cooking spray.
2. Cut beef round steak into 1 inch strips, and place in the slow cooker.
3. Add green pepper, onion, broth, and dressing mix.
4. Cover and cook on low for 7-8 hours, or on high for 3-4 hours.
5. Spoon meat mixture onto bread, and top with a slice(s) of cheese.
6. Another option is to toast bread in a 375 degree oven for 5-10 minutes,
7. Add meat, cover with cheese, then bake an additional 5 minutes to melt the cheese.
8. Add A1 sauce, and you're good to go (optional).

THE REVIEWS

SEE IT, RENT IT, OR BOOTLEG IT

See It, Rent It, or Bootleg It is our Siskel and Ebert moment. Basically, this is how it works. If a movie is worth the ticket price, food, and parking, then we say see it! If it's not really worth the money, but you still want to be able to say you saw it when questioned at the barbershop, then bootleg. When a movie is pretty much a waste of hard drive space, we wait it out, and add that bullshit to your Netflix list.

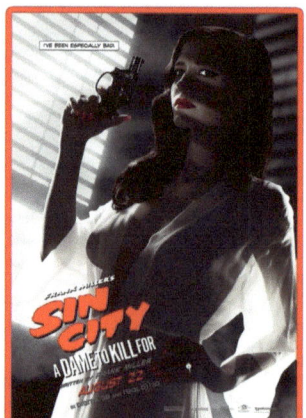

SIN CITY 2: A DAME TO KILL FOR

Starring: Eva Green, Jessica Alba, Bruce Willis, Rosario Dawson, Mickey Rourke, Josh Brolin

Sin City 2 is the ultimate spin on modern film noir. It has everything a growing boy needs: blood, guts, and sexy babes! What more can you ask for? Robert Rodriguez and Frank Miller together again: Bonus! The original Eva Green movie poster (On the Let): Satisfaction!

RECOMMENDATION: SEE IT

Also See It:
Into the Storm, When the Game Stands Tall

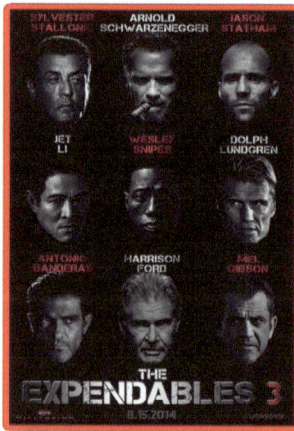

THE EXPENDABLES 3

Starring: Sylvester Stallone, Jason Statham, Aronold Schwarzenegger, and just about every non-working action hero you can think of...

Look, I grew up watching action movies starring all of these bad ass mofos! However, can we stop for a moment and ask ourselves: How many action heros can we fit into one movie! Geesh! The Expendables franchise brings more old men out of retireemnt than a Viagara sample party!

RECOMMENDATION: BOOTLEG IT

Also Bootleg It:
Guardians of the Galaxy, Let's Be Cops

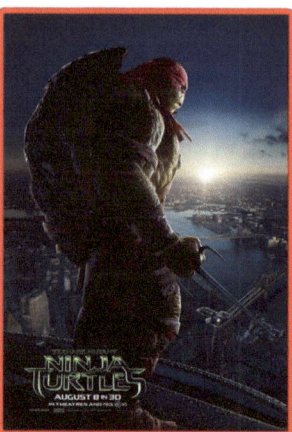

NINJA TURTLES

Starring: Johnny Knoxville, Alan Ritchson, Noel Fisher, Jermy Howard & Megan Fox

Oh! So, Mr. Michael "I Have More Money Than God To Make A Movie" Bay is doing the Turtles. I'm good. If Ninja Turtles turns out to be anything like the self absorbed sideshow of the Transformers Series, I'll pass. Just because you have $250 Million to make a movie doesn't mean you're going to make a great movie.

RECOMMENDATION: RENT IT

Also Rent It:
The Prince, The Novemeber Man

A GOOD BOOK

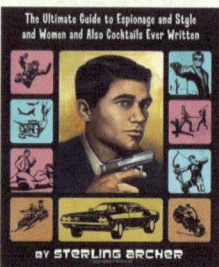

HOW TO ARCHER
by Sterling Acher

Lying is like 95% of what he does. But believe me: in this book, he will let you know exactly how to become a master spy just like Archer. Obviously, you won't be as good at it as he is, but that's because you're you, and he is Sterling Archer. - *$9.60*

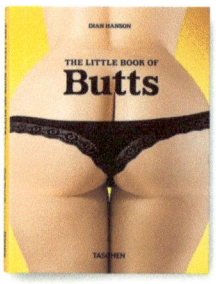

THE LITTLE BOOK OF BUTTS
by Dain Hanson

How can we pack so much big booty into such a tiny and inexpensive package? Sorry, but it's a trade secret we can't divulge, except to say that shoehorns and spandex were involved. The original Big Butt Book featured a great cross-section of delectable rears from the 1950s to the present day. Here, in the Little Book of Butts, since life is such an ironic deal, we decided to pare the original content down to just the biggest and the best, in-your-face phatties to which the great Sir Mix-A-Lot alluded when penning, "My anaconda don't want none, unless you've got buns, hun." - *$9.00*

THE ONE MOVIE THAT WILL GET YOU LAID - We feel your pain. It's movie night, and you forced your girl to see, "Rise of the Plant of the Apes" last month. Here's a suggestion, take her to see, **"If I Stay"** starring everyone's favorite kick-ass crime figther, Chloe Grace Moretz. True, she doesn't do any ass kicking in this movie, but the romantic tragedy will cetainly beat the tears of out of your girlfriend getting you right to the bottom - the bottom on your girlfriend's panty line.

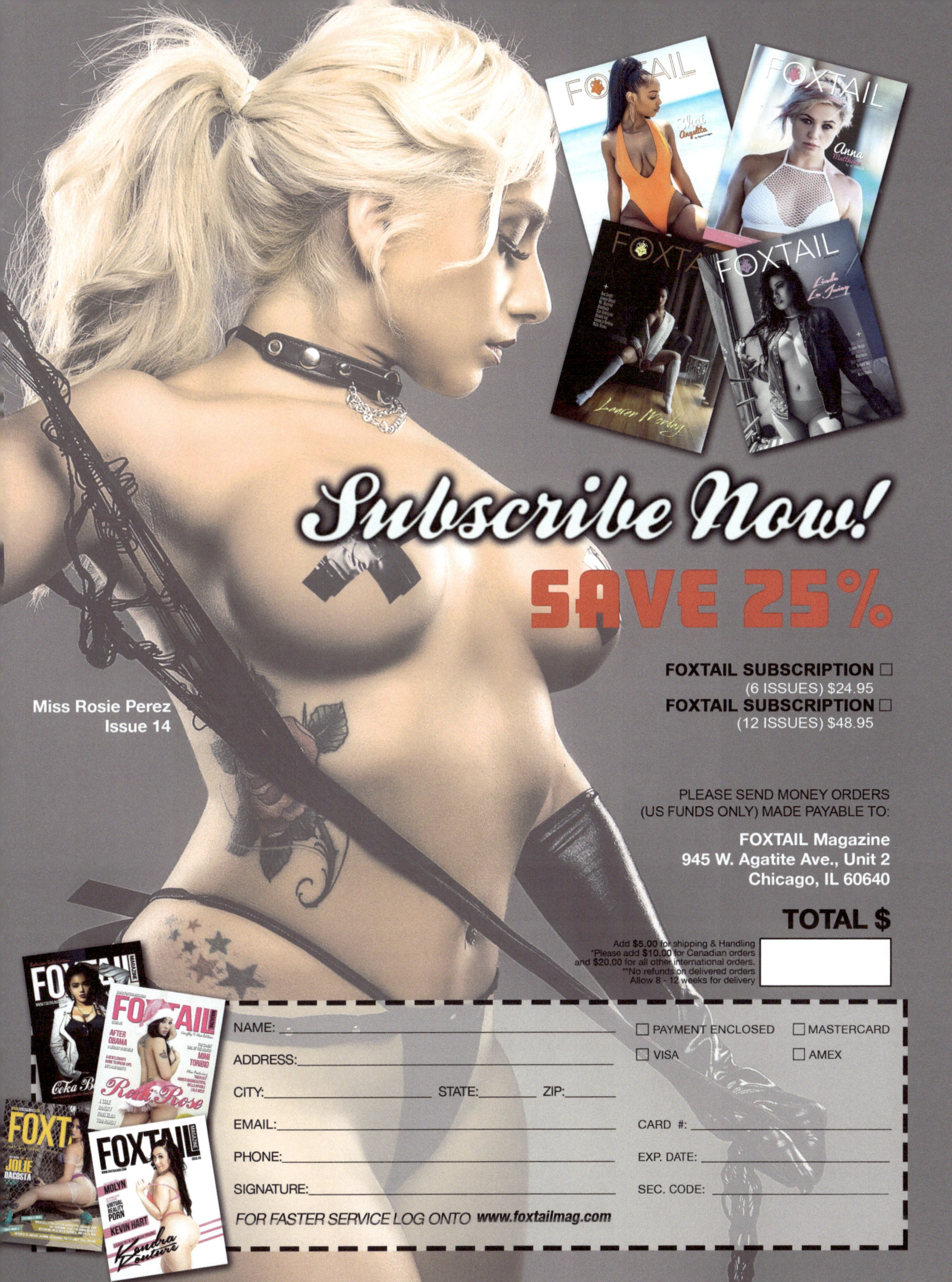

GET **FOXTAIL** MAGAZINE
On the Devices that Matter to You the Most!!!

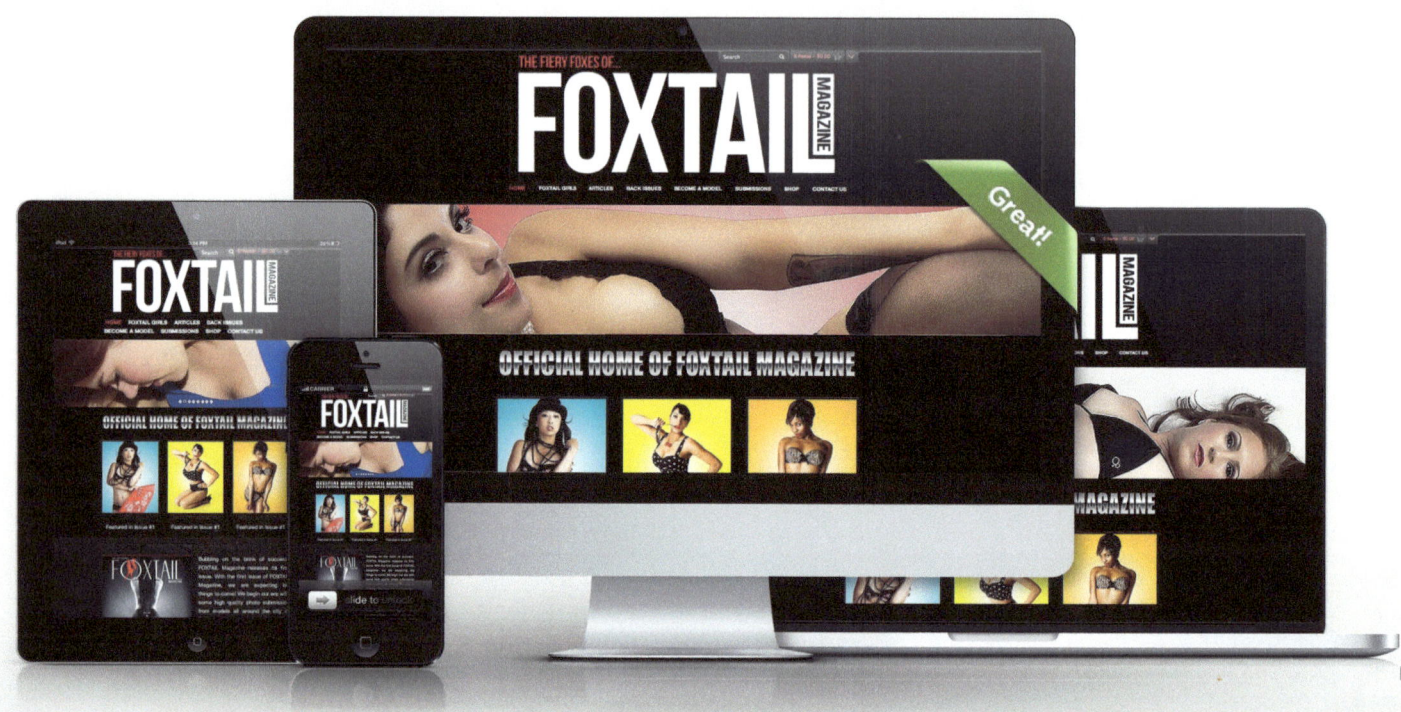

ADVERTISE
WITH
FOXTAIL MAGAZINE

FOR MORE INFOMATION SEND EMAIL TO: ADVERTISING@FOXTAILMAG.COM

www.ingramcontent.com/pod-product-compliance
Lightning Source LLC
Chambersburg PA
CBHW040409220526
45473CB00004B/1178